Managing the Environment the 14001 Way

Second Edition

David Smith and Clive Green

BSI
Business
Information

Second edition first published in the UK in 2005

by
BSI
389 Chiswick High Road
London W4 4AL

First edition published in the UK in 1999

Typeset in Great Britain
Printed in Great Britain by TJ International, Padstow, Cornwall

The FSC logo identifies products which contain wood from well-managed forests certified in accordance with the rules of the Forest Stewardship Council. Text printed on FSC certified paper supplied by Denmaur Papers. Cover printed on recycled board.

Mixed Sources
Product group from well-managed forests and recycled wood or fiber
www.fsc.org Cert no. SGS-COC-1885
© 1996 Forest Stewardship Council

British Library Cataloguing in Publication Data
A catalogue record for this book is available from the British Library

ISBN 0-580-45871-7

Managing the Environment the 14001 Way

Contents

Acknowledgements

The authors would like to particularly thank Chris Millidge for his assistance in reviewing and updating this book and also the input from David Robinson of BSI Management Systems and William Young of Leeds University School of Earth and Environment.

The authors would also like to thank their long-suffering partners Di and Andrea for the pressure that this and the previous publications have caused to their lives while the authors completed this work.

David Smith would like to take this opportunity to recognize the contribution made by the late John Mason who passed away in 1997. John was thoroughly committed to environmental management and advised the author on the business benefits to organizations.

Foreword

Organizations of all kinds are facing an intensifying and worldwide pressure from society and other stakeholder groups to achieve and demonstrate sound environmental performance. Controlling the impact of their activities, products or services on the environment is a major challenge for all managers. The environmental management standards produced by the International Organization for Standardization (ISO) help organizations meet this challenge.

BS EN ISO 14001:2004, *Environmental management systems – Specification with guidance for use* [1] (referred to as ISO 14001) specifies those requirements for an Environmental Management System (EMS) that may be objectively audited for certification/registration purposes and/or self-declaration purposes. The first edition published in 1996 had an amazing uptake and by 2005 the numbers of registrations has risen to about 70,000. There are many other organizations in the process of seeking certification or who have chosen to adopt the approach without seeking formal recognition. The second edition builds on this success by improving its understanding and effectiveness in implementation. It contains important changes and emphasizes points that may not have been elaborated sufficiently. For some organizations the impact of these changes will be quite minor, for others it may need far more extensive work to ensure their EMS is updated to meet the new requirements.

To provide assistance to organizations implementing or improving an EMS, BS ISO 14004:2004, *Environmental management systems – General guidelines on principles, systems and supporting techniques* [2] (referred to as ISO 14004) also came into effect in December 2004. In the UK, BS 8555:2003 [3] was published to help organizations to implement ISO 14001 using a phased approach. Guidance on auditing an EMS [4] has also been published (ISO 19011:2002), which shows that a common approach can be adopted to auditing BS EN ISO 9001:2000, *Quality management systems – Requirements* [5] (referred to as ISO 9001) and ISO 14001 systems

Managing the Environment the 14001 Way was first published in 1999 and is intended for organizations seeking practical help in developing a cost-effective EMS based on ISO 14001 and ISO 14004. It builds on the basic framework and principles of these standards by providing practical advice, examples, and sources of further information. There are also lists of commonly applicable environmental legislation and regulations. It is not intended, however, to be a comprehensive guide to all aspects of environmental management.

Managing the Environment the 14001 Way will be helpful to those organizations seeking to integrate an EMS within an overall formal management system (such as one based on ISO 9001 for managing quality; or OHSAS 18001:1999 [6] and BS 8800:2004 [7] for managing occupational health and safety). It recognizes the close similarities between managing environmental issues and managing occupational health and safety.

Managing the Environment the 14001 Way is not a stand-alone guide. Readers are directed, where necessary, to ISO 14001, ISO 14004 and other standards in the ISO 14000 series for additional information. Any definitions in ISO 14001 and ISO 14004 also apply.

Managing the Environment the 14001 Way does not in any way alter or amend limitations on the use of ISO 14001 and ISO 14004. Compliance with ISO 14001 and ISO 14004 does not in itself confer immunity from legal obligation.

1

Introduction

Organizations can no longer afford to ignore environmental pressures. Changing weather patterns around the world fuel an almost daily news debate about climate change. Global warming and global dimming are being attributed to human activities. Greenhouse gas emissions are a major concern and the burden of evidence is such that most informed bodies agree that the 'Precautionary Principle' needs to be applied to human activities that adversely impact on the environment. The announcement in 2005 of the commitment by many countries to the Kyoto Agreement is another manifestation of the importance that the world attaches to improving environmental management.

No organization can ignore its responsibility for managing the impact of activities, products and services on the environment. Increasingly stringent legislation, the pressure from society and customers, the development of economic policies and other measures to foster environmental protection, and a general growth in concern surrounding environmental matters, including sustainable development, produce an overwhelming case for performance improvement. The International Organization for Standardization (ISO) is currently drafting a guidance document on social responsibility (embracing environmental issues as one of its core elements) in response to the pressure on organizations to develop sustainable policies. This is mirrored by a guidance document on sustainable development in the UK.

In a competitive world adoption of the ISO 14001 approach may be seen as just an additional cost. However, there are many examples of substantial benefits accruing through savings on waste, and customer recognition. In addition, those organizations who adopt it freely without seeking formal recognition give further testament to the fact that ISO 14001 is seen as a sound business tool. The systematic evaluation and management of environmental impacts can bring with it business benefits through:

- improving operational efficiency;
- gaining competitive advantage;
- improving risk management;
- reducing liabilities (including insurance risks);
- avoiding adverse publicity;
- improving business performance; and
- gaining public recognition and showing commitment to the environment.

Organizations may have 'mission statements' committing themselves in broad terms to managing environmental issues. Indeed, many have undertaken environmental 'reviews' or 'audits' to assess their performance. On their own, however, these may not be sufficient to provide an organization with the assurance that its performance not only meets, but also will continue to meet its legal and policy requirements. To be effective, they need to be conducted within a structured management system and be integrated with overall management and business decision-making activities and processes.

An environmental management system (EMS) enables an organization to establish and assess the effectiveness of its internal management practices, to set an environmental policy and objectives, to achieve performance improvements and to demonstrate its environmental commitment to others. The ultimate success of the system depends on commitment from all levels and functions within the organization, but especially from top management.

Many organizations have already implemented one or more formal management systems (for instance, to manage quality and/or occupational health and safety) and are seeking to embrace these within one business or risk management system. Organizations decide themselves the extent to which they wish to interface or integrate their systems to improve their business focus and avoid unnecessary bureaucracy and duplication of paperwork. An approach is given that should allow organizations to integrate their separate systems into a single integrated management system (IMS).

Managing the Environment the 14001 Way explains how the various elements in developing and maintaining an EMS can be tackled. The book uses three fictitious organizations – an office environment, an engineering workshop and a retail operation – to show the parallels that exist between these very different work situations, and how the same basic principles can be applied to all types of organization.

The ISO 14001 approach is based on the Deming cycle – **P**lan, **D**o, **C**heck and **A**ct (PDCA). This is illustrated in Figure 1 of ISO 14001. The Initial Environmental Review, Policy and Planning fall under the heading of 'Plan'. 'Do' is the 'Implementation and Operation' stage and the other phases follow as would be expected in this continual improvement cycle.

How to use this book

For those wishing to build an EMS based on ISO 14001, following the book through page by page allows a comprehensive system to be developed. However, to allow further flexibility for others with more particular needs it also uses a combination of:

- *key element sections* – providing information on the key elements in ISO 14001;
- *in detail sections* – providing more detailed information;
- *in practice sections* – showing how the system can be implemented in practice, using the three fictitious organizations;
- checklists – providing a reference point to help identify how your organization compares with ISO 14001 and where you may need more detailed information;
- cross-referencing to ISO 14001 – providing an easy reference to the corresponding clause in the standard.

For those organizations with an EMS already in place

Some organizations will have an EMS in place, but they may either wish to reassure themselves about their system or may already recognize that there are specific deficiencies that need to be addressed. In this case it may help to fast track through the book by using the 'key element' sections and checklists to help to identify how your organization compares, and where you require more detailed information. You can then refer to 'in detail' sections, as necessary, or the checklists, which will help you to identify where you need to refer to the main text.

There is also a self-assessment questionnaire in Appendix 1, which will help you to assess your present EMS.

For new starters who want to get the basics in place quickly

For those with little or no system in place, ISO 14001 may seem a little daunting. There are no shortcuts to success. However, the approach in this book is such that it enables the new starter to identify the key elements that need to be addressed quickly. You can proceed to the other elements later, when time and resources permit.

The key thing to remember is that you must institute arrangements to control your significant environmental aspects. A good way to start is:

1. carrying out an initial environmental review (Chapter 2);
2. planning (Chapter 5);
3. identifying significant environmental aspects (Chapter 6);
4. defining an environmental policy (Chapter 3).

For small organizations

It is recognized that the whole process of establishing an EMS may appear overwhelming to a small organization, which is likely to have few environmental issues associated with its activities. The aim should be to address those environmental aspects that are present, managing them at a level appropriate to their significance and the size of the organization.

'Carrying out an Initial Environmental Review' (Chapter 2) and 'Identifying Significant Environmental Aspects' (Chapter 6) will enable you to ascertain the key elements of the system to concentrate upon. However, it is essential you cover the planning stage before carrying out a full evaluation of the environmental aspects of your organization.

The 'key element' sections in the other stages will then help you to decide the extent of the management system that will meet your particular needs. The way to proceed is:

1. carry out an initial environmental review (Chapter 2);
2. identify significant environmental aspects (Chapter 6);
3. plan (Chapter 5);
4. identify significant environmental aspects in detail (Chapter 6);
5. define an environmental policy (Chapter 3);
6. follow the key element sections of the remaining elements.

In practice – Background to the case studies

In order to help understand how implementing ISO 14001 might work in practice, three fictitious organizations have been considered. Any resemblance to any actual organization is purely coincidental. A background to each organization is given below to give the reader a feel for the situation as it exists. The examples and the approach will have many common features for all organizations, although there will always be some uniqueness about an individual organization's situation.

Floggit & Leggit (F&L)

Introduction

F&L is a 17-strong firm of accountants, established in 1985 by four partners who previously practised separately. Throughout the boom years of the late 1980s, it expanded rapidly to become a firmly established business in the centre of Leeds serving the UK and Europe. F&L has recently moved from old-fashioned offices to a modern, designer-built two-storey office suite on a business development park.

In its early days, occupational health and safety (OH&S) rarely featured in the organization's thinking and environmental management was of no interest whatsoever. Effective OH&S management has now been fully embraced within F&L and even those doubting the need have been surprised at the business benefits arising, however, F&L has still to consider environmental management.

Implementing an Environmental Management System

F&L's attitude to environmental management changed when a major client decided that they wished to include environmental accounting in their annual statements. They asked F&L if it had anyone who could audit this, and also whether F&L itself had an environmental policy. The partner who originally questioned the need for OH&S management immediately asked, 'What has environmental management got to do with an office?'. The other partners were less sceptical, and reflected on the benefits that the client had gained through reduced insurance, improved staff morale, and so on, when an effective OH&S management system was introduced. It was obvious that this was an important issue to the client, and perhaps they should look at it a bit more closely before dismissing it as irrelevant to them.

The partners decided that they should carry out a similar initial review to the one they performed when they implemented the OH&S system.

Unbespoke Engineering (UE)

Introduction

UE is an established engineering organization tracing its roots back to World War I when it began manufacturing rivets, nuts and bolts for war production. The early premises, two small wooden shacks, have since developed into a five-hectare site, with 83 employees, manufacturing high quality fasteners and precision gear mechanisms for the motor trade. Raw material is transported to the site for conversion into the finished product before being transported to a predominantly UK and European market.

The business activity is clearly defined into two categories: clerical/managerial support and manufacturing. The manufacturing side involves the use of precision engineering tooling and is undergoing a programme of replacement, modernization and computerization. The plant facilities are of relatively modern manufacture (circa 1980) and have been reasonably maintained. Manufacturing includes a number of processes apart from machining, including cleaning and preparation, and painting before dispatch to customers.

UE was used to dealing with probing questions from customers about quality and occupational health and safety, and was able to reassure them about the robustness of its management systems. Although it had been dealing adequately with questions on environmental issues on a piecemeal basis, nobody had overall responsibility for environmental management.

Implementing an Environmental Management System

UE was using a number of processes that needed to be controlled within various Acts and Regulations. The adoption of ISO 9001 had helped to formalize UE's management arrangements and to strengthen its procedures and documentation; it therefore seemed the ideal platform to build upon. The Quality Control Manager (QCM) was asked to take responsibility for this area of the business. The QCM soon realized, however, that the scope of environmental management was much broader. The arrangements for environmental management could not be embraced within the existing quality management system as this only covered two manufacturing processes.

UE set up a small team chaired by the QCM, which included the Purchasing Manager, the Plant Manager and the Health and Safety Adviser. UE had recently established an OH&S management system and was naturally keen to develop any opportunities for using common systems. UE decided that using an ISO 14001 approach was the most likely way to minimize potential duplication and bureaucracy.

Low Cost Discount (LCD)

Introduction

LCD has been trading since 1979, supplying a full range of cut-price food and household products. It occupies a single-storey 200,000 square metre store with a car park on a 1970s shopping estate. The retail activity is supported by an administrative function and is serviced by a large warehouse area handling and storing incoming goods.

LCD was aware of the movement in the retail market towards 'green' products but, despite the protestations of an Assistant Manager, the Store Manager was confident that customers were more attracted by aggressive discounting. In view of this, LCD had concluded that environmental issues were not an immediate consideration in its business.

Over a period, LCD had been bothered with complaints from local residents about litter, and these have even led to the Local Authority threatening prosecution. Although LCD did not provide the customary skips outside for customers to return bottles and cans, this did not deter some from returning their empties, and this in turn was attracting more litter.

The threats had reached a level where it was no longer possible to ignore them, as they were beginning to impinge on other aspects of the relationship between LCD and the Local Authority. Finally, fearing that it might also begin to affect turnover, the Store Manager gave the 'green' Assistant Manager the task of solving the problem.

Implementing an Environmental Management System

Being 'younger and more enlightened than the boss' the Assistant Manager felt that this problem was symptomatic of the low-key attitude of LCD towards stocking environmentally friendly products. While investigating how other businesses were dealing with litter control, and after speaking to the local Chamber of Commerce, the Assistant Manager was impressed by the proactive way some were approaching a wide range of environmental issues – not just those relating to their choice of product range.

The Store Manager was persuaded that the litter control problem should be a catalyst for a wider look at how LCD dealt with environmental issues. The Assistant Manager pointed out how others were managing these issues for the benefit of their businesses. Also, by tackling this within the framework of ISO 14001, as some local businesses had done, this would help to gain credibility with the Local Authority.

2

Carrying out an Initial Environmental Review

To many organizations, managing environmental issues will be relatively new compared to other areas such as production, quality, finance and occupational health and safety. The first important step in establishing an effective EMS is to carry out an initial environmental review.

The review helps organizations find out:

- where they are now in managing environmental issues;
- what needs to be done;
- what help and information is available from outside sources.

Before starting, it is important to clarify what is meant by some of the terms used. More detailed explanation will appear later on in the text but to help with this review the following terms need to be considered:

- environment – surroundings in which an organization operates, including air, water, land, natural resources, flora, fauna, humans, and their interrelation;
- environmental policy – overall intentions and direction of an organization relating to its environmental performance as formally expressed by top management;

- environmental management system – part of an organization's management system used to develop and implement its environmental policy and manage its environmental aspects;
- environmental aspects – element of an organization's activities, products or services that can interact with the environment;
- environmental impact – any change to the environment, whether adverse or beneficial, wholly, or partially resulting from an organization's environmental aspects.

There is no actual requirement in ISO 14001 to carry out this review for certification/registration purposes, although it is recommended for those organizations that do not have any environmental management system in place. Should you wish to seek recognition from a certification body you will need to demonstrate that you have a full appreciation of your environmental impacts. At the outset you have to find out, therefore, what the system needs to cover, and any legal requirements with which your organization needs to comply. Annex A of ISO 14001 (A.1) provides the following guidance:

An organization with no existing environmental management system should, initially, establish its current position with regard to the environment by means of a review. The aim of this review should be to consider all environmental aspects of the organization as a basis for establishing the environmental management system.

The review should cover four key areas:

a) identification of environmental aspects, including those associated with normal operating conditions, abnormal conditions including start-up and shut-down, and emergency situations and accidents;
b) an identification of applicable legal requirements and other requirements to which the organization subscribes;
c) an examination of all existing environmental management practices and procedures, including those associated with procurement and contracting activities;
d) an evaluation of previous emergency situations and accidents.

Identifying significant environmental aspects is covered separately (see Chapter 6), as it is a vital element in establishing an EMS.

At the outset it is important to decide the scope of the review. Depending on the time and resources available, this can range from a staged approach, concentrating first on specific operations or specific sites and extending to others later, through to a complete review of all the activities of the organization.

Legislative and regulatory requirements

Controls over environmental issues have been around for a long time, but it is only recently that tough UK and European legislation has been introduced covering most of the activities that lead to pollution. There are also a number of international conventions that apply worldwide that have to be met. At the other end of the scale local by-laws, public rights of way, or covenants, may affect the activities undertaken at a site.

In effect, legislation and regulation places a 'duty of care' on organizations to manage their resources well and to minimize pollution. You may think that none of this could possibly apply to you but, for instance, any organization, without exception, that generates waste of any sort has a legal responsibility.

Appendix 2 shows how to identify the regulations that apply to your particular business.

Checklist 2.1 covers some of the major legislation that applies across a broad spectrum of organizations. A tick box is provided for you to identify those that apply to your organization [1]; may apply [2]; or are irrelevant [3].

CHECKLIST 2.1: Legislation and regulations that may apply to your organization

1	2	3	
			Air Pollution
❑	❑	❑	*Clean Air Act 1993*
			Environmental Protection Act 1990
			Pollution Prevention and Control Act 1999
❑	❑	❑	**Energy**
❑	❑	❑	Buildings Regulations 2000
❑	❑	❑	**Land**
			Environment Act 1995
			Environmental Protection Act 1990
			Countryside and Rights of Way Act 2000
			Noise
❑	❑	❑	Anti-Social Behaviour Act 2003
			Control of Pollution Act 1974
			Environmental Protection Act 1990
			Noise Act 1996
			Noise and Statutory Nuisance Act 1993
			Pollution
❑	❑	❑	Environment Act 1995
			Environmental Protection Act 1990
			Pollution Prevention and Control Act 1990
			Waste
❑	❑	❑	Environment Act 1995
			Environmental Protection Act 1990
			Water
❑	❑	❑	Water Act 2003
			Water Industry Act 1991
			Water Industry Act 1999
			Water Resources Act 1991

Each of these principal Acts is supported and amplified by regulations dealing with specific aspects. Regulations which apply to your business can be identified as explained in Appendix 2.

In practice – Application of primary legislation and regulations

F&L – Office

Legislation applying includes:

- Environmental Protection Act 1990 Part 2 – Duty of Care Regulations 1991 (applies to the waste generated on site).
- Town and Country Planning Act 1990 (applies because the development of the site is very strictly controlled due to its close proximity to residential property).
- Various OH&S regulations that have environmental implications, e.g. Control of Substances Hazardous to Health regulations 1988 (COSHH) because of the use of chemicals for cleaning purposes.

At first sight there is little legislation that applies to F&L. However, they identified that they were in breach of the 'duty of care' (discussed in Chapter 6 – In Practice). Apart from being a significant environmental aspect for F&L, it was also a significant embarrassment to their image as a highly reputable professional organization. F&L addressed the problem immediately, and with great discretion, on the same day that it came to light. The commitment of all the partners to move on environmental management was thus quickly established.

UE – Engineering workshop

Legislation applying includes:

- Environmental Protection Act 1990 Part 1 (applies because of the emissions to air).
- Environmental Protection Act 1990 Part 2 – Duty of Care Regulations 1991 (applies because of the disposal of waste from processes).

- Environmental Protection Act 1990/93 – Noise and Statutory Nuisance Act (there were some concerns about the emissions from the site – which had given rise to public complaint in the past).
- Water Resources Act 1991(applies because of the discharge of effluent to a surface water drain).
- Water Industry Act 1991 (applies because of the discharge of trade effluent to a foul sewer).
- COSHH (applies because of the use of chemicals for cleaning, etc.).
- Special Waste Regulations 1996 (applies because of the disposal of empty cleaning chemical containers); will be the Hazardous Waste Regulations – plus they may well require a permit for the storage of Hazardous Waste.
- Notification of Cooling Towers and Evaporative Condensers Regulations 1992 (applies because of the cooling system).

An organization with a manufacturing base is more likely to attract a wide range of legislative and regulatory controls, and needs to examine its processes and activities closely to identify those that might apply.

UE discovered a contravention of the Water Resources Act when it carried out its initial environmental review and identified its environmental aspects (see Chapter 6). This also raised other concerns, such as the cooling system and whether there was a need for registration.

LCD – Retail

Legislation applying includes:

- COSHH (applies because of the use of chemicals for cleaning, etc.).
- Environmental Protection Act 1990 Part 2 – Duty of Care Regulations 1991 (applies because of the waste generated on site, other than packaging, from the fresh meat and bakery operations).
- Environmental Protection Act 1991 Part 4 (covering the control of litter).
- Producer Responsibility Obligations (Packaging Waste) Regulations 1997.

- Town and Country Planning Act 1990 (applies because the development of the site was very strictly controlled because of its proximity to residential property).
- Water Industry Act 1991 (applies because of the generation of trade effluent, i.e. cleaning water from the bakery/meat processes).

In an operation involving totally different types of activities, retailing, office and warehousing, LCD needs to identify any legislative and regulatory controls that may apply to each type of activity.

LCD was surprised to find that other legislation – Environmental Protection Act Part 3: Noise and Statutory Nuisance – might apply if it failed to manage its litter problem.

Existing practices, procedures and information within the organization

This involves looking at the existing environmental management practices, procedures, guidance, instructions and information that you already have within the organization. It also includes evaluating the results of investigations into any previous accidents and/or incidents.

Almost certainly there will be something in every organization. All organizations have to establish, at least, some arrangements to cover the disposal of waste. Details on disposal are normally included in the information provided by suppliers, and this will probably have been acted upon within the organization. There are also likely to be arrangements for transfer notices, waste consignment notes and for defining the nature of the waste to the licensed waste carrier. If the activities of the organization involve emissions to the atmosphere or discharges to watercourses, there should be licences or exemptions in place covering them. If the activities involve a significant use of materials there should be information from suppliers on the safe use and disposal of their products.

Checklist 2.2 shows some of the environmental management practices, procedures and information likely to be found in organizations, even though a formal EMS may not be established. A tick box is provided for you to identify those that already exist [1]; may apply [2]; or are irrelevant [3].

CHECKLIST 2.2: Existing environmental management practices, procedures and information in your organization

1	2	3	
❑	❑	❑	Waste disposal/licenses/transfer notes/guidance notes
❑	❑	❑	Licences for discharge to watercourses
❑	❑	❑	Licences for discharge to sewers
❑	❑	❑	Licences for emission to atmosphere
❑	❑	❑	IPC and LAAPC licences (including new requirements for release inventory) – IPPC will apply
❑	❑	❑	Emergency arrangements
❑	❑	❑	Fire emergency arrangements
❑	❑	❑	Noise control
❑	❑	❑	Provision of environmental requirements in procurement procedures
❑	❑	❑	Approval of operational procedures
❑	❑	❑	Health and safety risk assessments
❑	❑	❑	Safety policy
❑	❑	❑	Accident/incident reports
❑	❑	❑	COSHH – information/data sheets. Use of hazardous materials.
❑	❑	❑	CHIP
❑	❑	❑	Environmental training – competence
❑	❑	❑	Environmental training – induction (awareness)
❑	❑	❑	Security arrangements
❑	❑	❑	Storage arrangements
❑	❑	❑	Town and Country Planning information, public registers/planning consents, environmental statement for sites/projects subject to the EIA Regulations
❑	❑	❑	Historic information on the use of the site
❑	❑	❑	Historic information on processes previously used
❑	❑	❑	Communications with interested parties
❑	❑	❑	Information from the Local Authority on local environmental issues
❑	❑	❑	Information from trade associations

❑ ❑ ❑ Information from suppliers/subcontractors
❑ ❑ ❑ Information from plant/equipment suppliers
❑ ❑ ❑ Use of resources
❑ ❑ ❑ Availability of records

In practice – Existing practices, procedures and information within the organization

F&L – Office

Although the environmental impacts of an office operation are, generally, relatively small, F&L still need to identify these and ensure that they are being effectively managed.

Documentation likely to be available within an organization similar to F&L, and which may help in the initial environmental review, includes:

- COSHH assessments;
- Fire emergency procedures;
- Emergency arrangements;
- Safety policy;
- Occupational health and safety risk assessments;
- Town and Country Planning information from the Local Authority;
- Disposal of waste;
- Utilities bills for energy and water, stationery, office equipment.

UE – Engineering workshop

UE is likely to have some long-standing environmental aspects that it will have recognized already. Its level of awareness and control is likely to be greater than in the case of F&L, but, on the other hand, the consequence of poor management could be very damaging to the environment and expensive for UE. Failure to identify and manage some of their significant environmental aspects could conceivably put their longer-term future at risk.

Documentation likely to be available within an organization similar to UE, and which may help in the initial environmental review, includes:

- Accident/incident reports and investigations;
- Information from suppliers;
- Information from plant/equipment suppliers;
- Waste disposal guidance and instructions;
- Emergency arrangements;
- Fire emergency arrangements;
- Induction training procedures;
- Operational control procedures;
- Noise assessments;
- Packaging procedures;
- Preventative maintenance;
- Safety policy;
- Occupational health and safety risk assessments;
- COSHH assessments;
- Contractors and visitors procedures;
- Storage requirements;
- Procurement procedures;
- Utility bills for energy and water use.

LCD – Retail

In an operation involving totally different types of activities, retailing, office and warehousing, LCD needs to address environmental aspects in each part of the business. While, generally, the environmental impacts will tend to be small, the interface with the public does add a dimension that needs to be carefully considered.

Documentation likely to be available within an organization similar to LCD, and which may help in the initial environmental review, includes:

- Accident reports and investigation;
- Contractors and visitors procedures;
- Fire emergency procedures;
- First aid procedures;
- Induction training procedures;
- Preventative maintenance;
- Safety policy;
- Security arrangements;
- Disposal of waste;
- Procurement procedures;
- COSHH assessments;
- Occupational health and safety risk assessments;
- Packaging procedures;
- Storage requirements;
- Recycling arrangements;
- Procedures for returning 'empties' to suppliers;
- Litter control;
- Complaints;
- Correspondence with stakeholders;
- Utility bills for energy and water use.

Best practice and guidance from external sources

This covers any voluntary codes of practice and regulations, external standards and other benchmarks to which the organization subscribes and compares its performance. It also includes any guidance and instruction available from organizations and trade associations operating and/or specializing in similar fields of activity.

Very few processes and activities found in organizations are either so new or novel that there is no information about them. Information is readily available from many easily accessible sources and time spent here may pay dividends later in ensuring an effective EMS.

Trade associations, Green Business Clubs and similar bodies exist to support and coordinate technical developments within specific business sectors. Many produce information, advice and guidance focused on their particular sector. This is especially valuable as it is invariably based on the real-time experience of other member organizations. Similar information can arise out of a consensus between several different operators seeking to set voluntary standards within a particular sphere of activity.

The Environment Agency (EA) is an important source of information and should not be overlooked because of its regulatory role. The EA is keen to work with organizations to meet common goals of good environmental management and welcomes their contact. Useful publications from the EA include:

- Guidance Notes for integrated pollution control and for processes subjected to air pollution control;
- Technical Guidance Notes (TGNS) on monitoring, dispersion and abatement;
- Waste Management Papers (WMPS) offering guidance on regulations on waste, special wastes, licensing and packaging;
- Environmental Technology Best Practice Programme – helpline and publications.

The Health and Safety Executive (HSE) may be similarly useful, as there is often a close relationship between environmental and occupational health and safety issues. For instance, the series of HSE Guidance Notes will be particularly useful for organizations handling 'special' materials.

Local Authorities are another important source of information and support, not only related to their responsibilities for environmental health, but on issues such as the layout of land and buildings. For example, the Planning Guidance Notes provide guidance on the design of industrial and commercial developments and small firms. Appendix 2 gives more detail on sources of information.

Checklist 2.3 shows some possible sources of information on best practice and guidance. Tick boxes are provided for you to identify those that are relevant [1]; may apply [2]; or are irrelevant [3].

CHECKLIST 2.3: Sources of best practice information and guidance for your organization

1	2	3	
			Environment Agency
❑	❑	❑	*Guidance Notes*
❑	❑	❑	*Technical Guidance Note Series*
❑	❑	❑	*Waste Management Papers*
❑	❑	❑	*General Information*
			Health and Safety Executive
❑	❑	❑	*Guidance Notes*
❑	❑	❑	*General information*
❑	❑	❑	**Trade associations or similar bodies**
			Local Authority
❑	❑	❑	*Environmental Health*
❑	❑	❑	*Planning*
			Business Development Organizations
❑	❑	❑	*Chambers of Commerce*
❑	❑	❑	**Insurer/Insurance broker**
			Suppliers
❑	❑	❑	*Equipment*
❑	❑	❑	*Materials*
❑	❑	❑	*Services*
❑	❑	❑	**Customers**
❑	❑	❑	**Fire Officer**
❑	❑	❑	**Landlord**
❑	❑	❑	**Local environmental groups**

☐ ☐ ☐ **Environmental protection groups** *(Greenpeace, Friends of the Earth)*

☐ ☐ ☐ **Libraries**

Publications/Journals

☐ ☐ ☐ *ENDS Report*

☐ ☐ ☐ *Environment Business Magazine*

☐ ☐ ☐ *Industrial Environmental Management*

Professional bodies

☐ ☐ ☐ *Institute of Environmental Management*

☐ ☐ ☐ *Institute of Environmental Assessment*

In practice – Best practice and guidance from external sources

UE – Engineering workshop

UE best demonstrates the usefulness of outside sources for information on best practice and guidance. The engineering sector is particularly well served by trade associations and the information available from suppliers. Other sources include:

- Register of environmental regulations from the Engineering Employers Federation;
- 'CBI means business' publications (Confederation of British Industry) and other similar publications;
- DTI/DEFRA publications on waste minimization.

3

Defining an Environmental Policy

Under ISO 14001 the environmental policy is the only document you *have* to make publicly available, so it is important to get it right.

The environmental policy is the driver for implementing and improving an organization's EMS so that it can maintain and improve its environmental performance. It establishes an overall sense of direction and sets the level of environmental commitment, responsibility and performance expected of the organization.

The policy statement should reflect the organization's mission, vision, core values and beliefs. It should be an indicator of its aspirations, its intended behaviour, and the ethics that guide its decision-making.

Although there is no legal obligation to produce an environmental policy statement, as there is under the HASAW for occupational health and safety, many organizations may already have 'mission' statements committing themselves in very general terms to managing environmental issues effectively.

To develop a successful EMS a 'mission' statement alone is insufficient. In order to ensure delivery of this very general declaration, the organization needs to support it with more detailed policy statements, together with objectives and targets to implement it in practice.

From the outset, it is essential that there is support at the highest level within the organization for the EMS. Top management must fully endorse and sign the policy statement because its commitment and leadership is paramount in ensuring the policy statement's successful implementation.

ISO 14001 (4.2) specifies seven requirements to develop a comprehensive environmental policy statement.

1. The policy statement should be appropriate to the nature, scale and environmental impacts of the organization's activities, products and services

The policy statement must be relevant to the particular circumstances of the organization. If the organization operates in a high-risk field that has major impacts, this needs to be reflected in the policy. It also needs to be kept up to date and should be reviewed periodically and revised to reflect changing conditions and information.

It is impossible to formulate a policy statement without prior knowledge of the organization's environmental aspects and associated impacts. Information and data gathered during the initial environmental review (see Chapter 2) and the identification of significant environmental aspects (see Chapter 6) are crucial to deciding the specific issues that are to be included.

2. It should include a commitment to continual improvement and prevention of pollution

Society's expectations are increasing the pressure on organizations to reduce the environmental impact of their activities; more specifically, to prevent pollution, reduce waste, reduce the use of resources (materials, fuel and energy), and commit to recovery, re-use and recycling of resources. For instance, issues such as CO_2 emissions and global warming may need to be addressed in the selection and use of transport.

The overall aim should be to improve environmental performance by continually evolving the management system.

Suppliers, users and contractors should be encouraged to adopt a similar stance so that the complete product/service chain reduces its overall environmental impact. Remember that the environmental impact of a product or service is the sum of the impacts throughout its supply chain.

3. It should include a commitment to comply with applicable legal requirements, and with other requirements to which the organization subscribes that relate to its environmental aspects

Compliance with environmental legislation and regulations should be the minimum goal. Anticipating more stringent controls, however, by seeking to exceed these requirements is likely to be more sensible and prudent in the long run. Similarly, by tracking UN and European legislation 'in the pipeline', organizations can anticipate new legal requirements, avoiding the need for 'unplanned investment' in new plant or processes.

Many organizations adopt voluntary codes and practices and these should be viewed in the same way as regulatory compliance. For example, if your organization operates in the chemical sector and is a member of the Chemical Industries Association (CIA), it will need to include the requirements of the CIA's Responsible Care programme within its EMS.

4. It should provide the framework for setting and reviewing environmental objectives and targets

Ideally the policy statement should be kept brief, clear and concise to enable it to be easily understood by both internal and external parties. But it also needs to contain an appropriate level of detail to provide the framework for the setting of objectives and targets within the management system.

Often policy statements and objectives are unrealistic because inadequate and/or inappropriate resources are available to deliver them. The policy statement should make commitments that allow identifiable and attainable objectives to be set. Before making any public declarations the necessary finance, skills and staff empowerment must be available, and all targets should be realistically achievable within this framework.

To avoid possible embarrassment, it is important also that the environmental policy is consistent with other existing policy commitments and decisions within the organization. For example, the existing policies on ethics, finance, human resources, procurement, quality and occupational health and safety needs to be considered.

5. It should be documented, implemented and maintained

ISO 14001 does not require the organization to keep large volumes of paperwork. Documentation should be appropriate to the needs of the organization and sufficient to enable it to deliver its policy.

Involving employees is often neglected. In much, if not all, of industry, employees wish to make a positive contribution. They understand that the cost of unnecessary waste reduces competitiveness in the market place and that a pollution incident brings adverse publicity. At the end of the day, they recognize that environmental aspects need to be managed cost-effectively in order to maintain the security of their employment and the quality of their working environment and the local community from which many of them will come.

6. It should be communicated to all persons working for or on behalf of the organization

Clause A.2 of ISO 14001 explains that communication of the policy to contractors 'can be in alternative forms to the policy statement itself, such as rules, directives and procedures, and may therefore only include pertinent sections of the policy'.

Communication should, where necessary, involve training to ensure that employees are competent to undertake any tasks they are required to perform. Training should be tailored to meet business demands and supported by appropriate refresher courses to maintain standards.

In organizations undertaking project or development work, designers need to be aware not only of present risks but also about possible future risks that may be posed if they do not consider environmental impacts at the planning and design stage.

7. It should be available to the public

There is a need to recognize the views and concerns of interested parties when developing a policy statement. This communication process should take on board local interest groups as well as the more influential stakeholders, such as investors and regulators. Local communities are often overlooked by organizations, but employees and local inspectors who live there may be especially concerned about issues affecting the local area and region. The local community may also have information on the past uses of a site that is relevant to the organization's consideration of its environmental aspects.

Enlightened organizations recognize the need to be proactive in communicating their policy to others. They reissue the policy statement on an annual basis to let stakeholders and other interested parties know how the business is performing against its policy objectives, targets and legal obligations.

Checklist 3.1 asks key questions about your present policy statement. A tick box is provided for you to identify those issues that you already cover and those you need to consider.

CHECKLIST 3.1: The policy statement in your organization

Yes	No	
❑	❑	Does top management approve the policy and has a senior manager been allocated overall responsibility for implementing it?
❑	❑	Does it guide the setting of environmental objectives and targets to implement it in practice?
❑	❑	Do you make available adequate and appropriate resources to implement it?
❑	❑	Do you ensure that your policy is understood, implemented and maintained at all levels in your organization?
❑	❑	Do you periodically review your policy to take account of changing circumstances, and carry out audits to ensure that its implementation is effective?
❑	❑	Do you ensure that your employees and sub-contractors receive appropriate instruction and training and are competent to carry out any duties and responsibilities necessary to implement the policy in practice?
❑	❑	Do you take into account the views of employees?
❑	❑	Do you take into account the views of other interested parties, including local interest groups?
❑	❑	Do you make the policy available to all interested parties and the general public?
❑	❑	Do you adequately reflect the relevant significant environmental impacts of your activities, products or services?

- [ ] [ ] Do you commit yourself to complying with relevant environmental legislation and regulations, and with all other requirements to which you subscribe?
- [ ] [ ] Do you commit yourself to continual improvement and prevention of pollution?

4

Creating a Climate for Effective Environmental Management

Some organizations appear to have effective systems on paper (or electronic form) that are fully comprehensive, and yet in reality there is little commitment to deliver, while in performance terms the output is poor.

To achieve a positive culture that sustains a robust system that continually improves can be difficult. It often takes time to build up the trust of the workforce. It is hard to ensure that supervisors and managers do not subscribe to good practices only when it is convenient and then forget everything when they have to meet challenging production targets. All too often, major problems occur because the culture has not been embedded in those working at the operational level. One disenchanted worker leaving a tap running, or carelessly disposing of waste, can cause major problems in environmental impact terms and on the reputation of the organization.

The culture of an organization is very much influenced by its leadership. It is difficult to develop a positive culture for one particular discipline, but the risks within the business may well ensure there is a strong focus in one area. This should be used to cascade the commitment to all activities. If an organization shows a caring attitude to the welfare of employees, then the employees are far more likely to embrace good practices in order to help the organization.

The problems are very similar to those encountered in implementing an occupational health and safety system, and the following management system guidance given in BS 8800:2004 is equally applicable in the environmental field:

a) staff is committed to the aims of their organization, and the way the organization is managed;
b) top management and senior staff demonstrate visible EM commitment, including their personal behaviour, showing leadership by example. They make it clear that they are keen to hear the bad news as well as good news and they will take action on the information they receive;
c) senior staff and supervisors spend time discussing and promoting good environmental and waste management practices; commend good environmental behaviour and express concern if procedures are not being followed;
d) EM is managed with the same determination as other key business objectives;
e) EM and waste management is a normal topic of day-to-day discussion in the workplace and there is active feedback on performance.

Equally there are many factors that can impair the culture, e.g.:

a) inconsistencies in rules and procedures;
b) supervisors and managers not acting upon non-compliances with rules, e.g. when there is a production emergency;
c) rules and procedures developed without due consideration for their practicability;
d) rules and safeguards imposed by external agencies and consultants that do not take into account the complexity of the operation and the challenges of compliance;
e) failures to communicate shortcomings in EMS arrangements;
f) suggestions for improvements or changes from employees are not welcome and/or are not acted upon;

g) there is no employee involvement in, for instance, risk assessment, developing operating procedures or carrying out incident investigations;
h) there is an acceptance that violations are inevitable, and that little can be done to eliminate them;
i) a culture of blame exists;
j) underestimation of the magnitude of risk for any reason.

There is no quick way to overcome lack of commitment. This has to be gained by promoting good practices such as those given in the first list above. It is essential to involve members of the workforce, asking their views on what needs to be done.

In the environmental field, it is easy to promote interest and gain commitment by involving employees in identifying opportunities for improvement and developing new approaches that give environmental benefits.

5

Planning

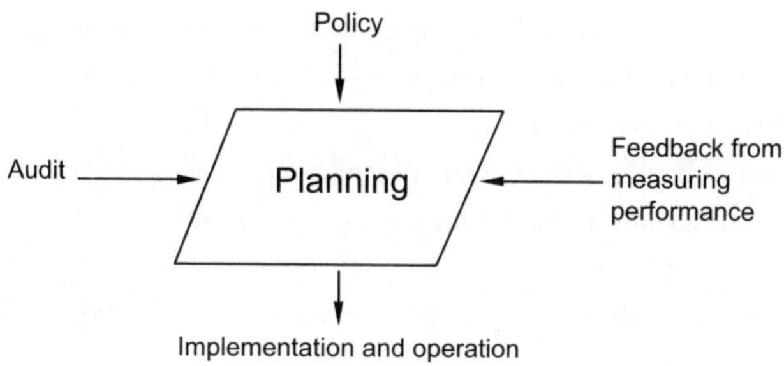

Figure 5.1

Key Elements – Planning

Planning for EMS involves:

identifying requirements for the system	–	what needs to be done;
setting clear performance criteria	–	what is to be done;
allocating responsibility	–	who gets it done;
setting time scales	–	when it is to be done by;
identifying the desired outcome	–	what the result should be.

ISO 14001 (4.3) identifies three key areas that need to be addressed during the planning stage:

1. environmental aspects;
2. legal and other requirements;
3. objectives, targets and programme(s).

1. Environmental aspects

The organization shall establish, implement and maintain a procedure(s)

a) to identify the environmental aspects of its activities, products and services within the defined scope of the environmental management system that it can control and those that it can influence taking into account planned or new developments, or new or modified activities, products and services, and

b) to determine those aspects that have or can have significant impact(s) on the environment (i.e. significant environmental aspects).

The organization shall document this information and keep it up to date.

The organization shall ensure that the significant environmental aspects are taken into account in establishing, implementing and maintaining its environmental management system. (4.3.1)

Procedures need to be regularly updated to reflect changes in legal requirements, regulatory control and the expectations of interested parties. For those organizations that use plant, machinery and equipment there is a clear need to identify and use the best available technology where this is economically viable, cost-effective and appropriate.

Procedures also need to recognize the environmental impact that suppliers, contractors and customers may have that could have an adverse effect on the environmental probity of the organization.

The process of identifying environmental aspects and evaluating associated environmental impacts is central to the planning process and, ultimately, the success of the EMS. (See Chapter 6.)

2. Legal and other requirements

The organization shall establish, implement and maintain a procedure(s)

a) to identify and have access to the applicable legal requirements and other requirements to which the organization subscribes related to its environmental aspects, and

b) to determine how these requirements apply to its environmental aspects.

The organization shall ensure that these ... are taken into account in establishing, implementing and maintaining its environmental management system. (4.3.2)

There has been a significant change in the 2004 standard with respect to the phrase 'applicable legal requirements'. This means that legislation such as COSHH needs to be considered because it has environmental issues such as how to deal with spillages within its requirements.

'Other requirements' include industry codes of practice such as the Chemical Industries Association's *Responsible Care*, or a voluntary code such as Investors in People. There are a number of sources where information can be obtained on current legislation, as well as keeping track of changes (see Appendix 2 for more information). It is important to be aware of legislation that may be under consideration at international, European, national and even local level. Failure to do so may mean that recently installed plant soon becomes redundant or that you have to invest quickly in new equipment or materials for which there is no budget provision.

Simply being aware of legislation is not sufficient – the organization needs to understand the implications of it for them and what is required to meet its obligations.

The role of contractors or suppliers working on behalf of the organization, whose actions can affect compliance, should not be overlooked.

3. Objectives, targets and programme(s)

The organization shall establish, implement and maintain documented environmental objectives and targets, at relevant functions and levels within the organization.

The objectives and targets shall be measurable, where practicable, and consistent with the environmental policy, including the commitments to prevention of pollution, to compliance with applicable legal requirements and with other requirements to which the organization subscribes, and to continual improvement.

When establishing and reviewing its objectives and targets, an organization shall take into account the legal requirements and other requirements to which the organization subscribes, and its significant environmental aspects. It shall also consider its technological options, its financial, operational and business requirements, and the views of interested parties. (4.3.3)

Clear and attainable objectives together with specific and measurable targets answer the question – how do we get to where we want to be? They translate the commitments in the environmental policy into the goals against which environmental performance is compared.

Measurable environmental performance indicators should be selected as the means for evaluating and comparing performance against objectives, targets and other criteria in order to demonstrate continual improvement (see Chapter 8 for more information).

Objectives and targets should be regularly reviewed and revised to reflect changing circumstances.

4. Environmental management programme(s)

The organization shall establish, implement and maintain a programme(s) for achieving its objectives and targets. Programme(s) shall include

a) designation of responsibility for achieving objectives and targets at relevant functions and levels of the organization; and

b) the means and time frame by which they are to be achieved. (4.3.3)

The environmental management programme is the mechanism by which environmental objectives and targets are met. An organization may choose to develop and implement more than one programme to achieve the same objective. Similarly, one programme may cover more than just one objective.

Ideally, the programme should be integrated within the organization's overall strategic plan to ensure that there are no conflicts of interest, and that the environmental impacts of any new projects and developments are taken into consideration before they are implemented. Other issues to consider when producing a programme are:

- involving all responsible parties in the planning process;
- ensuring it is responsive to changes in policy, objectives and targets;
- identifying actions and priorities;
- ensuring arrangements are in place to monitor and review it.

Checklist 5.1 identifies the main areas that need addressing. A tick box is provided for you to identify those procedures you already have in place [1], and those you need to introduce [2].

CHECKLIST 5.1: Planning in your organization

1	2	
		Environmental aspects
❑	❑	Programme(s) are in place to identify and evaluate the environmental aspects of the organization's activities, products and services (i.e. those that we can control or which we can be expected to have influence over).

☐ ☐ Significant environmental impacts associated with these aspects are considered in the setting of environmental objectives.

Legal and other requirements

☐ ☐ Procedures are in place to identify, track and understand environmental legislation, applicable regulations and other requirements to which your organization subscribes.

☐ ☐ These are considered in the setting of environmental objectives.

Objectives and targets

☐ ☐ These are consistent with the environmental policy.

☐ ☐ They are established and reviewed, taking into consideration available technology, financial requirements, operational requirements, business requirements and the views of interested parties.

☐ ☐ Environmental performance indicators are selected for measuring progress.

☐ ☐ They are regularly reviewed and revised, if necessary.

Environmental management programme(s)

☐ ☐ Programme(s) are in place for achieving environmental objectives and targets.

☐ ☐ The environmental management programme is integrated within the overall strategic planning process.

☐ ☐ Responsibility for achieving objectives and targets is clearly designated at the appropriate level(s) within the organization.

☐ ☐ Those responsible for achieving objectives and targets have sufficient knowledge, skill, authority, resources and time.

In practice – Planning

F&L – Office

F&L allocated responsibility for environmental management to the Office Manager. The immediate reaction was to focus on the usage of paper and to consider setting up recycling schemes. Someone said perhaps they should consider energy usage and this resulted in looking at the energy use in the new offices. Examination of the initial fuel bills showed that the cost of heating, lighting, etc., was a significant environmental aspect of the organization.

A programme was established to determine the reasons for the high energy use and report within one month to the Partners' Meeting, recommending ways of reducing energy use and its cost. This was to be followed by an action plan to implement any agreed recommendations such as improvements in the heating and lighting arrangements, changes in working practices, changes in types of fuel and suppliers, etc.

UE – Engineering workshop

The initial environmental review showed that there was no waste management strategy within the organization and that the effective management of its waste offered significant potential savings for UE. A programme was drawn up to establish the main sources and types of waste, including packaging, and the best way to manage them. A report was to be issued in six months' time.

LCD – Retail

The allocation of responsibility for environmental management to the Assistant Manager enabled a coordinated approach across the different activities in LCD. The first priority was to resolve the litter problem. It was found that providing arrangements for receiving bottles, cans and packaging could offer financial benefits as a recycling scheme, and was likely to be well received by customers. A small taskforce was set up, including a representative from the purchasing department, to determine, within three months, the type and location of disposal units, and the best financial package.

In detail – Planning

The ultimate success of an EMS depends on commitment from everyone working for or on behalf of the organization. Creating a climate for effective environmental management is discussed in Chapter 4.

Prior to beginning the planning process it is important to recognize that the EMS is likely to be more effective and contribute to improving overall business performance if:

- there is commitment from the outset at the highest level of the organization;
- it is an integral part of the overall management system;
- there is commitment to continual improvement of environmental performance throughout the organization;
- a proactive approach to environmental management is adopted;
- the process is ongoing and flexible to cope with changing circumstances, for example, new or amended legislation, changes in materials or processes, developments in technology, reorganization, staff changes;
- the process draws together all the relevant experience available to the organization in order to determine the best approach.

For all but the smallest organization a team-based or 'taskforce' approach is the best way forward. The taskforce should include representatives from all the functions in the organization affected by the EMS, and the senior manager responsible for environmental matters should ideally head the taskforce. This approach helps to spread the workload, and is more likely to gain commitment and support from those who will implement the EMS.

The size of the taskforce will depend on the organization, but it should be kept relatively small. Co-opting specialists when needed, or establishing sub-groups to deal with, say, particular activities, products, services or sites are ways of drawing in relevant experience without increasing the size of the core group.

Procedures should be put in place for providing regular progress reports to top management, those involved in the development process, as well as other employees and interested parties such as regulators, suppliers and contractors. This will help to retain commitment to the EMS. Where early 'quick wins' have been achieved (for example, fuel savings, reduced waste) this should be communicated to those concerned so as to maintain motivation and awareness.

Procedure for EMS planning

The procedure for EMS planning is no different from that which should be used to plan and implement change in any other aspect of your organization. The key stages in EMS planning are shown in Figure 5.2.

1. Drawing up a list of environmental objectives

This stage answers the question: how do we get to where we want to be? Time spent here pays dividends later in ensuring resources are targeted effectively, and that the organization prioritizes its efforts towards reducing its most significant environmental aspects.

The major sources of information for developing the initial list of environmental objectives are the:

- environmental policy (see Chapter 3);
- initial environmental review (see Chapter 2);
- process of identifying significant environmental aspects (see Chapter 6);
- legal and other requirements (see Chapter 2);
- management review (see Chapter 10).

Where external standards, such as regulatory requirements, either do not exist or do not meet the need, the organization can consider setting its own internal performance criteria.

Other sources of information include the views of interested parties, site plans, planning records, plant records, process records, audit reports, and accident and incident data. Input from employees who will be responsible for achieving the objective helps to gain commitment, as well as being an important source of local knowledge.

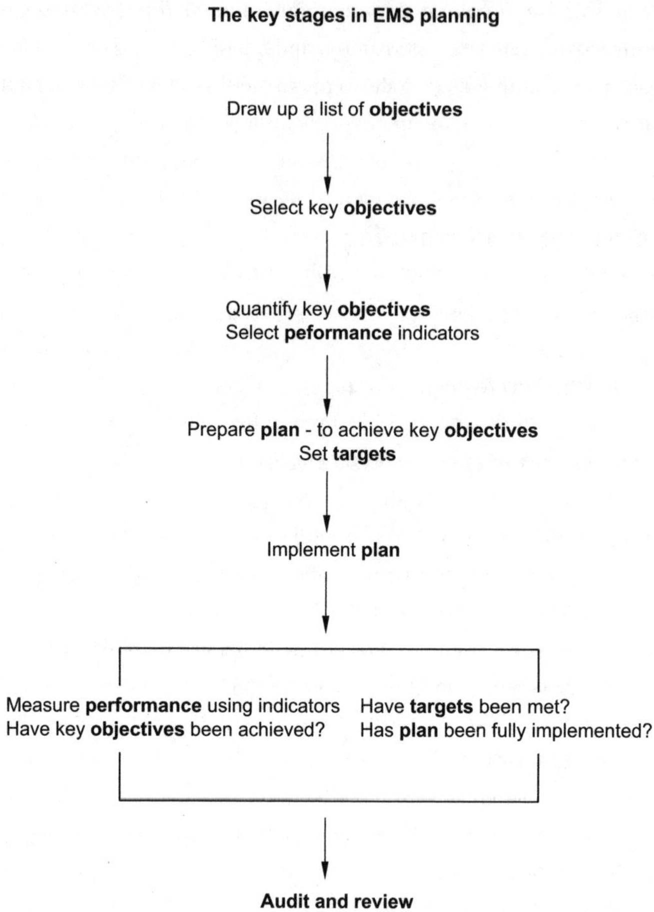

Figure 5.2

Please note that for completeness this figure also covers the implementation, checking, correcting and review stages; these are covered in Chapters 7–10.

The following 'guide words', shown with some examples, may be useful in formulating the wording of environmental objectives:

reduce – waste, use of natural resources, environmental incidents/accidents;
increase/improve – efficiency of material and energy use; use of recycled material in packaging; design of products to minimize their environmental impact;
introduce – environmental awareness programme; environmental aspect assessment, emergency response plan; waste recycling programme;
eliminate/substitute – use of specified hazardous substances, release of pollutants into the environment;
maintain/continue – use of materials from sustainable sources, use of non-hazardous substances.

2. Selecting key objectives

The next stage is prioritizing the objectives in the initial list to select those key objectives that match the environmental aims of the organization and the resources available.

When selecting objectives, it is important to make sure that they are specific, relevant and achievable in a reasonable period of time.

In developing an EMS, the organization is facilitating a change in its culture towards improving the management of environmental issues. Involving the workforce by concentrating first on those objectives that can be achieved easily and preferably at low cost helps build confidence and momentum (provided this is consistent with the prioritizing of environmental aspects). There are obvious benefits, if some of the objectives chosen give a positive financial return within one or two years. Such objectives encourage the organization to embrace environmental management as a valuable contributor to the business performance rather than a 'green' fringe item.

As commitment grows the more difficult areas can be taken on board.

3. Quantifying objectives and selecting performance indicators

The aim should be to set objectives, which, if at all possible, are quantifiable and can be measured. The point is often made that 'if you can't measure it you can't manage it'.

Using the same 'guide words' for objectives the following shows how these might be quantified:

reduce – specify a numerical figure and date for achievement;
increase/improve – specify a numerical figure and date for achievement;
introduce – specify a date for achievement;
eliminate/substitute – specify a date for achievement;
maintain/continue – specify existing level of activity.

In order to determine whether objectives are being achieved, it is good practice to select measurable performance indicators. Guidance on selecting performance indicators is given in Chapter 8.

4. Preparing plans to achieve key objectives by drawing up targets

The final stage in the planning process answers the question: how do we get there?

The broad content of the plan should be developed by breaking down the key objectives into the individual elements that need to be put in place such as training, consultation, communication and information gathering. For each element the plan should specify the detailed performance targets necessary to implement it:

who is to do **what**, by **when** and with what **result**.

The arrangements need to be such that they can be readily audited by an independent source.

Performance targets can be listed as a series of questions to act as a checklist for those responsible for achieving them. Whichever form is chosen they should be clearly drafted so that designated persons/teams know exactly what they have to do. Those who are to be allocated targets should be consulted about their practicality and be competent to undertake them. The documentation on targets can later be used to check progress on implementing the plan.

The resource implications of the plan should be considered. It should be costed and adequate financial resources made available to those assigned with the key responsibilities. The final plan will need to be fully resourced and taken forward with the complete support of senior management to ensure implementation.

6

Identifying Significant Environmental Aspects

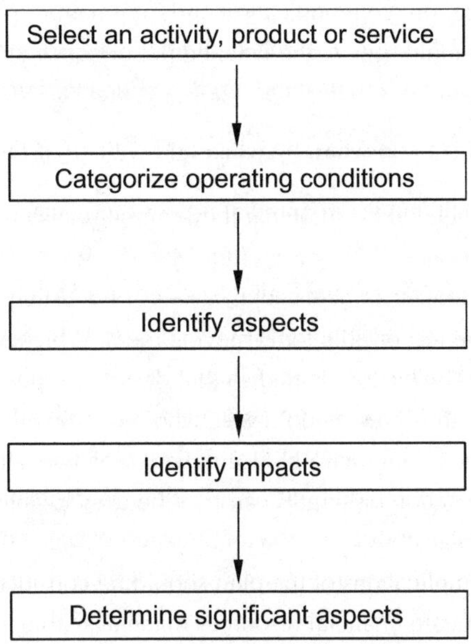

Figure 6.1

Key Elements – Identifying significant environmental aspects

ISO 14001 states:

The organization shall establish and maintain (a) procedure(s):

(a) to identify the environmental aspects of its activities, products and services within the defined scope of the environmental management system that it can control and those that it can influence taking into account planned or new developments, or new or modified activities, products and services, and

(b) to determine those aspects that have or can have significant impact(s) on the environment (i.e. significant environmental aspects).

The organization shall document this information and keep it up-to-date.

The organization shall ensure that the significant environmental aspects are taken into account in establishing, implementing and maintaining its environmental management system. (4.3.1)

The process of identifying environmental aspects and evaluating associated environmental impacts that arise from the activities, products and services of an organization is central to establishing a successful EMS. For organizations starting out, it is a vital element in establishing their current position during the initial environmental review (see Chapter 2). Organizations with an established EMS need to update, on an ongoing basis, the information on significant environmental aspects to ensure their systems continue to address priority issues. Changes or additions to activities, products or services, as well as changes in the priorities of the organization's stakeholders, such as investors, regulators and pressure groups, affect the environmental aspects and their associated impacts.

ISO 14001 defines the key terms in the process as:

Environmental aspect:
element of an organization's activities or products or services that can interact with the environment
NOTE: A significant environmental aspect has or can have a significant environmental impact.

Environmental impact:
any change to the environment, whether adverse or beneficial, wholly or partially resulting from an organization's environmental aspects

Annex A of the standard includes the following advice:

An organization should identify the environmental aspects within the scope of its environmental management system, taking into account the inputs and outputs (both intended and unintended) associated with its current and relevant past activities, products and services, planned or new developments, or new or modified activities, products and services. (A.3.1)

An organization needs to identify all those environmental aspects that it can control and over which it can be reasonably expected to have an influence (see Figure 6.2). This forms a sound basis for determining those aspects that can lead to the most significant environmental impact and that need to be addressed as priority issues within the EMS. Organizations should not focus only on their principal activities. For example, a forwarding company may find that its most significant aspects are those of its contracted transport suppliers.

The process should cover past, current or potential future environmental impacts (both positive and negative). It should also consider different operating conditions:

This process should consider normal operating conditions, shut-down and start-up conditions, as well as the realistic potential significant impacts associated with reasonably foreseeable or emergency situations. (A.3.1)

The methodology is similar to the approach used for managing occupational health and safety risks and relates to the way quality can be managed. This may especially benefit those organizations wishing to adopt common or integrated systems in these three key areas of management.

There are four stages in the process:

1. Selecting an activity, a product or service.
2. Identifying any environmental aspects associated with the selected activity, product or service.
3. Identifying any actual and potential, positive and negative, environmental impacts associated with each identified environmental aspect.
4. Evaluating the significance of each identified environmental impact.

ISO 14001 does not prescribe specific techniques for identifying environmental aspects or evaluating the significance of environmental impacts. Organizations can adopt those of their own choice.

Checklist 6.1 covers the procedures that need to be addressed in identifying significant environmental aspects. A tick box is provided for you to identify those procedures you already have in place [1], and those that you need to introduce [2].

CHECKLIST 6.1: Identifying significant environmental aspects

1	2	
❑	❑	Procedures are in place to identify all environmental aspects, i.e. those which can be controlled and influenced.
The procedures embrace all:		
❑	❑	activities
❑	❑	products
❑	❑	services
The procedures consider:		
❑	❑	normal operations
❑	❑	abnormal operations
❑	❑	potential emergency conditions

Procedures are in place to determine which environmental aspects:

☐ ☐ have had a significant impact on the environment (past)

☐ ☐ have a significant impact on the environment (present)

☐ ☐ can have a significant impact on the environment (potential)

☐ ☐ The information on significant environmental aspects is continually updated to take account of new activities, products, services, projects, etc.

☐ ☐ Significant environmental impacts are considered in the setting of environmental objectives and targets

In practice – Identifying significant environmental aspects

Although the three organizations have very different environmental impacts and adopt different processes to establish their significant environmental aspects, the overall approach should fundamentally be the same.

F&L – Office

The Senior Partner's view was that the major issue was paper and that introducing a recycling scheme would see F&L well along the way to implementing a sound EMS. However, the member of staff assigned with the responsibility of establishing the EMS decided that the review needed to be wider, covering all energy and material use, as well as waste generated by their activities.

The review quickly established a fundamental flaw in the way F&L handled waste. Although most of the waste was paper, F&L were relying on its contract cleaning company to empty the waste bins each night and to remove the contents from site. No one seemed to have determined the legality of this arrangement. It was not clear if the contract cleaners had a licence and whether any transfer notices were being issued. For all they knew, confidential information might be being dumped in a nearby wood. The scandal if this were to be the case could destroy F&L. This situation was addressed immediately.

The completed review showed that the most significant environmental aspects were the management of energy on site and the lack of a transport policy. The use of paper, apart from the handling of waste, was actually of less significance. In fact the total cost of paper used was only 10 per cent of the cost of energy used, and hence energy management offered a far greater opportunity for reducing the impacts as well as for saving money.

UE – Engineering workshop

The existing quality system was implemented using a failure mode and effects analysis approach. Each element of the process was considered to identify those that were critical in determining the quality of the product. The QCM decided to utilize the same approach for identifying environmental aspects, using a simple modified input/output model:

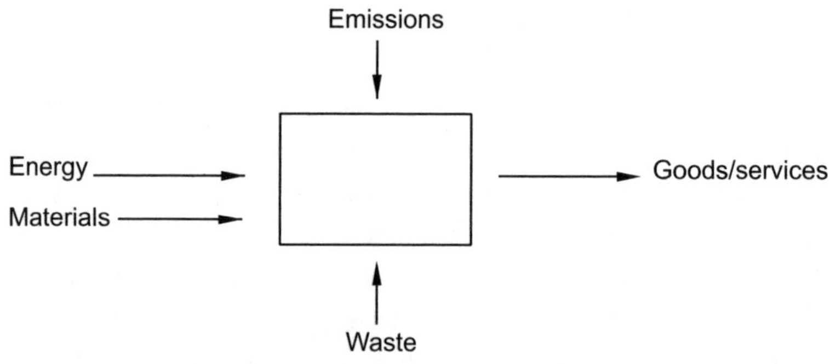

Figure 6.2

When all the environmental aspects were identified the impact of each was established using a matrix approach:

Activity/product/ service	Aspect	Impact
Activity – plating baths		
– discharge of effluent	Possible discharge above consent limits	Damage to sewage plant and possibly river life
– handling of hazardous chemicals	Potential for accidental spillage	Contamination of soil and/or natural waters
– storage of chemicals	Potential for accidental leakage	Contamination of soil and/or natural waters
– use of water	Lack of efficient control over a natural resource	Shortfall in water supply in an area traditionally short of natural supplies
– use of toxic chemicals	Potential for harm, e.g. in the community	Harm to the community by transfer of toxic materials from site to domestic situation
*Service – maintenance, etc. for plating baths**		
– cleaning baths and plating area	Potential for accidental spillage	Discharge of toxic gases to community
– disposal of waste	Incorrect disposal	Pollution of land, etc.

* This was a service provided by the suppliers of the process chemicals to UE.

The use and disposal of water was strictly controlled by the local water service company and was identified as a significant aspect in a number of UE's activities. In order to determine their compliance in this area, a comprehensive site survey was carried out by one of the maintenance fitters who had worked for UE for more than 20 years. UE identified that they were actually in breach of the law and were illegally discharging effluent at one point on their site.

UE also identified other environmental aspects that required further investigation to determine their significance:

- use of energy;
- use of toxic plating chemicals;
- use of paint solvents;
- waste management;
- the risk of legionella in the cooling towers.

LCD – Retail

The initial complacency of the Store Manager had been quickly dispelled when the Environmental Health Officer reminded him that the failure to control litter outside the store was an offence that could see him personally prosecuted and even imprisoned. This was obviously one significant environmental aspect that needed to be addressed quickly.

However, the Assistant Manager persuaded him that their approach needed to be wider and more systematic if they really meant business. The review subsequently identified the management of waste and the use of energy as significant environmental aspects for LCD. The Assistant Manager also identified the 'life cycle' aspect of packaging, bags, containers, etc., as a significant aspect, and the need to work with the suppliers and customers to reduce the impact of packaging materials. A waste audit was commissioned, using some assistance from external sources, to establish how the waste could be minimized or better managed.

The Assistant Manager suggested that she would appreciate some help and that she was aware that there was a local 'green' group who were looking to help organizations wanting to implement environmental schemes. The Manager was not too interested until he found out that the Local Authority would fund the project.

In detail – Identifying significant environmental aspects

Information on how to carry out this operation is available from a number of sources, some of which are listed in Appendix 2.

The process may be organized in the same way as an assessment programme carried out to identify risks associated with occupational health and safety. In this case activities, products or services are considered with respect to how they interact with the environment.

It is important to maintain the objectivity of the process and to maximize the information-gathering process, without causing too much disruption to the organization. The process necessitates gathering information from a number of sources, a site survey and interviews with key employees.

Checklist 6.2 identifies some of the key elements that should be considered in a programme for identifying significant environmental aspects. A tick box is provided for you to identify those elements you already have in place [1], and those that you need to address [2].

CHECKLIST 6.2: Requirements for an environmental aspects assessment programme

1	2	
❑	❑	Appointing a senior member of the organization to promote and manage the activity.
❑	❑	Consulting everyone involved; discussing what is planned to be done and obtaining their contributions and commitment.
❑	❑	Determining training needs for the assessment of environmental aspects and implementing a training programme if required.
❑	❑	Reviewing the adequacy of the proposed assessment scheme and determining whether the assessment is suitable and sufficient: that is, adequately detailed and rigorous.
❑	❑	Designing a simple pro-forma (or using an 'off the shelf' kit) to record the findings of an assessment, typically covering work activity; aspects; operational controls in place; administrative details, e.g. name of assessor, date, etc.
❑	❑	Documenting administrative details and significant findings of the assessment (hard copy or computer based if preferred).

The process

1. Selecting an activity, product or service.
2. Categorizing operating conditions.
3. Identifying environmental aspects of the activity, product or service.
4. Identifying environmental impacts.
5. Determining the significance of environmental impacts.

Note: ISO 14001 and ISO 14004 do not prescribe specific techniques for determining the environmental aspects of an organization, or for assigning significance. There are many schemes in operation and some have become more widely used because they apply more generally. However, at the end of the day it is up to individual organizations to decide what is appropriate for them and what they feel comfortable using. Should the organization seek certification they will, however, need to convince the assessors that their method is relevant, soundly based, consistent with their environmental policy, and capable of generating reproducible results. Obviously if the approach chosen identifies, for instance, that the use of paper is the most significant impact when they are operating in a recognized high-risk industry, the approach may be seen as flawed.

An alternative method is to use a staged approach to implementation, as described in BS 8555 *Guide to the phased implementation of an environmental management system* (3).

1. Selecting an activity, a product or service

ISO 14001 does not require organizations to carry out a detailed life cycle assessment or to evaluate every product, component or raw material input. Organizations may select categories of activities, products or services to identify those aspects most likely to have a significant impact. (A.3.1)

It is important that the selected activity, product or service is large enough for meaningful examination and small enough to be sufficiently understood.

In order to make the task more manageable activities or services may be classified or grouped in a convenient fashion such as by:

- geographical areas within/outside the organization's premises;
- stages in a production process, or in the provision of a service;
- planned work and reactive work (e.g. work carried out that is reacting to an unplanned event);
- defined tasks (e.g. driving, disposal of waste);
- identified working groups.

The process should not be restricted to core manufacturing or service activities and may need to consider support activities (e.g. cleaning) and administrative activities (e.g. energy and resource use).

The process should consider past, current and planned activities, products or services.

2. Categorizing operating conditions

Consideration should be given to all reasonably foreseeable operating conditions and any potential emergency situations:

Normal – the usual day-to-day operation of plant;
Abnormal – shut-down and start-up situations;
– maintenance situations;
– periodic increases in production capacity or the frequency of service delivery;
Emergencies – situations arising, say, from a chemical spill, flood or fire.

3. Identifying environmental aspects of the activity, product or service

The aim is to identify as many interactions as possible with the environment, both beneficial and adverse, associated with the selected activity, product or service.

When identifying the environmental aspects associated with the activities at operating units, ISO 14001 (A.3.1) suggests organizations should consider, where relevant:

a) emissions to air;
b) releases to water;

c) waste management;
d) contamination of land;
e) uses of raw materials and natural resources;
f) other local environmental and community issues.

There are a number of key questions that may help at this stage:

- Is there a source of harm to the environment?
- Who (or what) could be harmed?
- How could harm occur?
- Are there regulatory controls that apply to the activity?
- Is there significant expenditure on this service, material or product compared with the organization's turnover?
- Is this activity, service, material strictly controlled by the organization?
- Is the material from a sustainable source?
- Are significant amounts of energy, water, material used?
- Are significant amounts of waste produced?
- Have your customers challenged the use of materials or the environmental probity of your services?
- Have you received complaints from neighbours or the community at large about your impact on the environment?
- Does the location of the organization require special environmental consideration, e.g. is it close to a sensitive area?

The following list, though not exhaustive, gives examples of the information that can help to identify environmental aspects.

Identifying environmental aspects

1. Tasks being carried out – duration; frequency; permanence; timing (e.g. day or night).
2. Location(s) where the work/activity is carried out.
3. Who normally/occasionally carries out the tasks (e.g. maintenance).
4. Others who may be affected by the work (e.g. maintenance staff, visitors, contractors, the public, environment).

5. Training that personnel have received about the tasks.
6. Written systems of work/permits/procedures prepared for the tasks.
7. Plant, machinery and equipment that may be used.
8. Manufacturers' or suppliers' instructions for operation and maintenance of equipment, plant, machinery and powered hand tools.
9. Nature of materials/substances encountered.
10. Services used (e.g. compressed air, water).
11. Physical form of material used or encountered (fume, gas, vapour liquid, dust/powder, solid).
12. Concerns about the reducing availability of a specific resource.
13. Content and recommendations of hazard data sheets or material data safety sheets relating to substances used or encountered.
14. Requirement of Acts, regulations and standards relevant to the work being done, the plant and machinery used, and the substances used or encountered, including legislation in the pipeline.
15. Control measures believed to be in place.
16. Existing data: incident, accident and ill-health experience associated with the work being done, equipment and substances used, gained as a result of information from within and outside the organization.
17. Findings of any existing assessments relating to the work activity.
18. Complaints received on the activities carried out, or the resultant products or services.

4. Identifying environmental impacts

The relationship between an environmental aspect and an environmental impact is one of cause and effect – with an aspect leading to an impact or impacts. The aim is to identify as many environmental impacts as possible, actual or potential, positive or negative, associated with each identified aspect.

In theory, potential environmental impacts for some organizations may be almost infinite and ISO 14001 recognizes that you have to draw the line somewhere:

Organizations may take into account the degree of practical control they may have over the environmental aspects being considered. (A.3.1)

The organization is left to decide how far it extends its sphere of influence and where it draws the boundaries for its system. Determining the scope of the impacts to be considered should involve a clear evaluation of the role that the EMS is to play. Dealing with 'what you can get away with' is a futile process which is likely to reap very limited benefit for the effort expended. Even your customer's use of the product could be a significant aspect. For instance, would you, as a fertilizer manufacturer, want a customer who was using your product to make terrorist bombs?

In deciding whether or not an organization can be reasonably expected to have an influence over an environmental impact, the following questions may be useful:

- How far might the organization influence:
  - customer pressure?
  - investment in research and development?
  - information provision?
  - discussion?
  - financial pressure?
  - publicity?
  - other organizations in the supply chain?
- How much effort would it take to influence the impact?
- How effective are the attempts to influence likely to be?
- How much reduction in the impact(s) is likely to result?
- How significant are the impact(s) to the organization?

Environmental impacts can be categorized according to the environmental vectors that they affect:

- *greenhouse effect* (the stratospheric accumulation of some gases that may lead to climate change);
- *stratospheric ozone depletion* (degradation products of CFCs, etc., react with and destroy the stratospheric ozone layer, a function of which is to protect the earth's surface from excess UV sunlight);
- *natural resources* (consumption of non-renewable resources);

- *acid rain* (reaction of acidic ions with water in the atmosphere acidifies precipitation resulting in acidification of receiving waters);
- *surface water* (pollution of groundwater, rivers, lakes, estuaries and sea affects not only the ecosystem within those waters but also ecosystems that are dependent on them);
- *bioaccumulation of toxins* (some compounds persist in the environment leading to possible bioaccumulation and toxic effects);
- *local air quality* (local accumulation of airborne pollutants);
- *waste burden* (air/water/soil pollution caused by waste disposal);
- *external noise* (amenity impact on neighbours of noise and vibration);
- *soil and groundwater* (pollution of soil and groundwater);
- *ecological habitat* (loss of flora and fauna);
- *visual intrusion* (visual intrusion of major constructions).

5. Determining the significance of environmental impacts

The relative significance of the same environmental impact can vary between organizations and locations. What can be regarded as significant in one organization, may be considered trivial in another when compared to the range of other environmental impacts that are present.

Evaluating the significance of environmental impacts is a judgement that involves considering both environmental and business issues:

Environmental concerns include:

- the scale of the impact;
- the severity of the impact;
- the probability of occurrence;
- duration of the impact.

Business concerns include:

- potential regulatory and legal exposure;
- difficulty of changing the impact;
- cost of changing the impact;

- effect of change on other activities or processes;
- concerns of interested parties;
- effect on the public image of the organization.

Ideally, significance should be determined with reference to a combination of three factors:

1. environmental assessment of the impact;
2. financial considerations;
3. stakeholder priorities.

Financial considerations cover business and commercial repercussions for the organization arising from environmental liabilities and impacts (actual or potential).

Stakeholders include regulators, customers, investors, the local community and pressure groups. Organizations need to evaluate which stakeholder priorities are likely to be the most important to them. The requirements of regulators should be considered as a priority.

All three factors are subject to constant change. Understanding of the scientific issues upon which environmental impacts are judged evolves as more research and evidence becomes available. Stakeholder priorities are likely to respond to changing social attitudes and the level of environmental information available.

Developing a set of questions to apply to each identified environmental impact is a useful means of filtering out those that should be regarded as significant. Examples of questions are given below. The list is not exhaustive and organizations should develop a set of questions to reflect their own particular circumstances:

- Is it subject to legislative/regulatory control?
- Is it covered by any codes of practice or guidelines?
- Would the emergency services be involved if there were an incident?
- Does it have (or have the potential to cause) a demonstrable impact on the environment?

- Is it likely to cause complaints?
- Does it have financial implications?
- Could it result in financial/legal liabilities?
- Is it likely to be of concern to customers?

Information and guidance that may be of assistance in establishing criteria for determining significance are also available from a number of sources. These include:

- Regulatory permit/consent/authorizations and emission limits.
- Sector application guides.
- Guidance notes from regulators and industry associations.
- Environmental impact assessment reports and statements.
- Occupational health and safety reports and audits.
- Toxic release inventories and reporting.
- Stakeholder evaluation surveys.
- Scientific journals.
- Insurance company risk assessments.
- Independent audits/assessments.
- Environmental site assessments.
- Public registers, e.g. the planning register and the register of contaminated land maintained by Local Authorities.

Quantification can aid judgement. If a scoring technique is used, it is important to define any criteria, and to ensure the system is focused and consistent. It is important to avoid adopting a complex system that may overcomplicate the evaluation process. Simple is often best, and certainly more readily understood by interested third parties. Any scoring system used should be capable of providing reproducible results.

Scoring systems can be used in conjunction with risk assessment techniques to identify significant environmental impacts. The simple example shown below compares the level of hazard to the environment from the environmental impact with the performance of management in controlling the hazard.

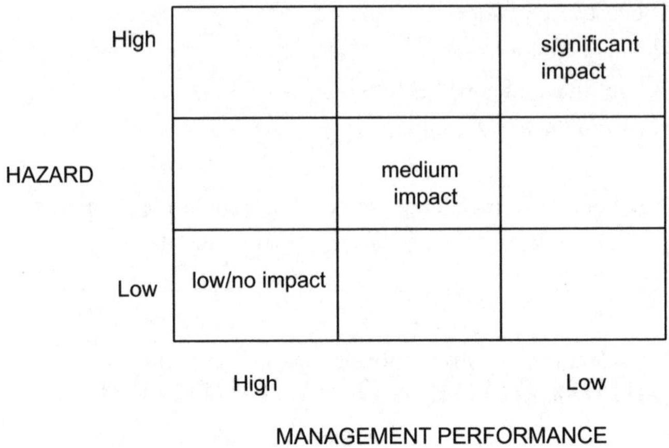

Figure 6.3

Criteria of management performance might include records of compliance, frequency of incidents and/or complaints, plant maintenance and operation, etc.

7

Implementing and Operating

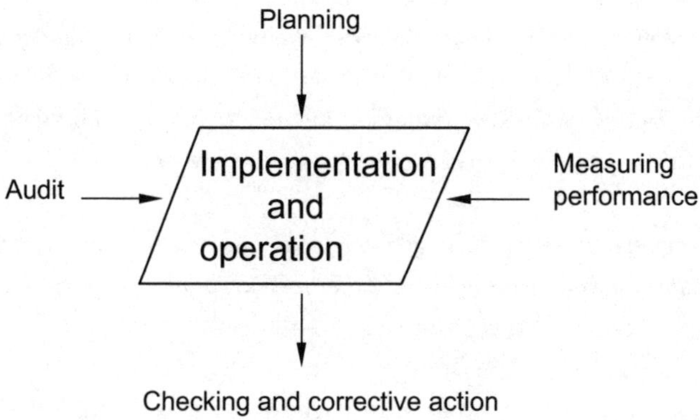

Figure 7.1

Key Elements – Implementing and operating

For successful implementation and operation of an EMS, ISO 14001 identifies seven key areas that need to be addressed:

1. Resources, roles, responsibility and authority.
2. Competence, training and awareness.
3. Communication.
4. Documentation.
5. Control of documents.
6. Operational control.
7. Emergency preparedness and response.

1. Resources, roles, responsibility and authority

Management shall ensure the availability of resources essential to establish, implement, maintain and improve the environmental management system. Resources include human resources and specialized skills, organizational infrastructure, technology and financial resources.

Roles, responsibility and authorities shall be defined, documented and communicated in order to facilitate effective environmental management.

Note that one of the key changes in the new standard is 'implement'. This is where this requirement needs particularly to be addressed.

The organization's top management shall appoint a specific management representative(s) who, irrespective of other responsibilities, shall have defined roles, responsibilities and authority for

a) ensuring that an environmental management system is established, implemented and maintained...;
b) reporting to top management on the performance of the environmental management system for review, including recommendations for improvement. (4.4.1)

To be successful, top management must show its commitment to and leadership of the EMS. Allocating responsibility to someone at a senior management level (e.g. in a large organization, a board or executive committee member) for ensuring the EMS is implemented and performing throughout the organization, sends a clear signal of this intent.

Responsibility and accountability must be clearly defined throughout the organization. Employees at all levels should be accountable, within the scope of their responsibilities, for environmental performance in support of the overall EMS.

2. Competence, training and awareness

The organization shall ensure that any person(s) performing tasks for it or on its behalf that have the potential to cause a significant environmental impact(s) identified by the organization is (are) competent on the basis of appropriate education, training or experience and shall retain associated records... (4.4.2)

All employees must receive sufficient training to undertake their responsibilities effectively and competently. Training should not just be seen as a 'one-off' given as part of the routine induction training when joining an organization. It should be refreshed and revised in the light of changing circumstances. Training needs exist at all levels within the organization. Top management need to be aware of the strategic importance of environmental management to ensure continued support and commitment. At the operational level, one error by an employee or a contractor can completely destroy an organization's credibility within a few seconds. Training should, therefore, be specific, ongoing and skill-enhancing to improve performance. Contractors are sometimes overlooked and should demonstrate that their own employees receive the appropriate level of training to conform to the policy of the organization they are working for. All employees and, where appropriate, contractors need to be aware of their individual and collective responsibility.

3. Communication

...the organization shall establish and maintain a procedure(s) for:

a) internal communication among the various levels and functions of the organization;
b) receiving, documenting and responding to relevant communication from external interested parties. (4.4.3)

Communication is important to demonstrate management commitment to dealing with environmental issues in a positive and proactive manner. Providing information helps to motivate employees, to facilitate public understanding and acceptance of the organization's position, and to inform public and regulatory authorities. The use of pictograms can be particularly effective.

Open communication is a two-way process: mechanisms should be encouraged, wherever possible, for responding to the concerns of employees and other interested parties. When encouraged, employees can often bring forward ideas that will bring both business and environmental benefits.

4. Environmental management system documentation

The environmental management system documentation shall include:

a) the environmental policy, objectives and targets;
b) description of the scope of the environmental management system;
c) description of the main elements of the environmental management system and their interaction, and reference to relate documents;
d) documents, including records, required by this International Standard; and
e) documents, including records, determined by the organization to be necessary to ensure the effective planning, operation and control of processes that relate to its significant environmental aspects. (4.4.4)

ISO 14001 does not require the organization to keep large volumes of paperwork. It is perfectly acceptable to use, say, the existing training record system rather than create one for the EMS.

The level of detail should be appropriate to provide a trail to the core elements and their interaction, and from where more detailed information can be obtained on the operation of specific elements of the EMS.

5. Control of documents

Documents required by the environmental management system and by this International Standard shall be controlled. Records are a special type of document and shall be controlled in accordance with the requirements given in 4.5.4.

The organization shall establish, implement and maintain a procedure(s) to

a) *approve documents for adequacy prior to issue;*
b) *review and update as necessary and re-approve documents;*
c) *ensure that changes and the current revision status of documents are identified;*
d) *ensure that relevant versions of applicable documents are available at points of use;*
e) *ensure that documents remain legible and readily identifiable;*
f) *ensure that documents of external origin determined by the organization to be necessary for the planning and operation of the environmental management system are identified and their distribution controlled; and*
g) *prevent the unintended use of obsolete documents and apply suitable identification to them if they are retained for any purpose. (4.4.5)*

Control over documentation is essential, but it is important that the organization focuses on effective implementation of the EMS, rather than on maintaining a complex, well-documented system. Emphasis should be on ensuring that the end user has access to accurate, up-to-date documents and is able to understand their content. This demands a level of personal literacy and may even require translation into other languages. When translation is necessary it is essential to ensure that the new document correctly interprets the original. An increasing number of organizations use computer networks to control their EMS documentation.

6. Operational control

The organization shall identify and plan those operations that are associated with the identified significant environmental aspects consistent with its environmental policy, objectives and targets, in order to ensure that they are carried out under specified conditions, by

a) *establishing, implementing and maintaining a documented procedure(s) to control situations where their absence could lead to deviation from the environmental policy, objectives and targets;*

b) stipulating the operating criteria in the procedure(s); and

c) establishing, implementing and maintaining procedures related to the identified significant environmental aspects of goods and services used by the organization and communicating applicable procedures and requirements to suppliers, including contractors. (4.4.6)

Establishing and maintaining operational procedures and controls are essential to ensuring that the organization's environmental policy, objectives and targets can be met.

It is important to remember the broader scope of the EMS. Apart from the day-to-day operational activities related to the core products and services, support functions such as research and development, purchasing, contracting, storage, transportation, marketing, etc., should not be overlooked. It is common to forget maintenance activities, especially those carried out infrequently, and facilities such as storage, interceptors, and bunding.

7. Emergency preparedness and response

The organization shall establish, implement and maintain a procedure(s) to identify potential emergency situations and potential accidents that can have an impact(s) on the environment, and how it will respond to them.

The organization shall respond to actual emergency situations and accidents and prevent or mitigate associated adverse environmental impacts.

... periodically review and where necessary, revise its emergency preparedness and response procedures, in particular, after the occurrence of accidents or emergency situations.

...periodically test such procedures where practicable. (4.4.7)

All organizations should have contingency plans to ensure that they have an appropriate response to mitigate any consequences arising from abnormal operating conditions or accidents and emergency situations. Contingency planning should also consider the environmental impact of accidental emissions, discharges and releases into the atmosphere, water and land. Ideally, an emergency plan pro-forma should be developed to help deal with accidents, etc.

Contingency plans should include the evacuation of employees and visitors, liaison with emergency services, clean-up measures and start-up arrangements when the incident has been successfully controlled or mitigated.

Checklist 7.1 identifies the key areas in implementing and operating an EMS. A tick box is provided for you to identify those procedures you already have in place[1], and those you need to introduce [2].

CHECKLIST 7.1: Implementing and operating an EMS in your organization

1	2	
		Structure and responsibility
❑	❑	A senior manager is allocated with full responsibility for the EMS throughout the organization
❑	❑	There is clear responsibility in the management structure
❑	❑	There is clear accountability in the management structure
❑	❑	There is clear delegation of authority in the management structure
❑	❑	All necessary resources are allocated
❑	❑	All employees are aware of their individual and collective responsibilities
		Competence, training and awareness
❑	❑	A competence, training and awareness assessment programme is in place
❑	❑	A retraining and refresher training programme is in place
❑	❑	A procedure to test the effectiveness of training is in place
		Communication
❑	❑	A system for effective, open communication of environmental information, internally and externally, is in place
		Documentation
❑	❑	An adequate documentation system is in place

Document control

☐ ☐ Documents are kept up to date and relevant

☐ ☐ All responsible personnel have access to appropriate documentation

Operational control

☐ ☐ A system of operational procedures and controls is in place, where necessary, to ensure that the objectives of the EMS are met

Emergency preparedness and response

☐ ☐ Contingency plans are in place for dealing with emergencies, incidents and abnormal operating conditions to mitigate the consequences, including any environmental impacts, arising from them

☐ ☐ A pro-forma checklist exists for dealing with emergencies

In practice – Implementing and operating

F&L – Office

To implement the plan for reducing energy use, F&L allocated specific responsibility to individual staff. Initially, the aim was to reduce energy by good housekeeping measures, including the use of light monitors, and timers for regulating heating. Weekly records were kept to monitor progress and savings.

UE – Engineering workshop

The survey of waste was implemented throughout UE under the stewardship of the Plant Engineer. The first stage was to establish an inventory of all materials ordered by UE and all the energy inputs to the site. The Plant Engineer found that the systems in place did not identify the electricity and water used by individual processes and was able to rectify this.

The next stage was to identify the source and exact nature of each type of waste. This turned out to be a difficult and tedious task and seemingly less than worthwhile, until the early results suggested there were a number of potential areas where significant savings could be achieved from reducing waste.

LCD – Retail

The implementation of the waste-recycling project was assigned to the Assistant Manager with responsibility for safety. This was to ensure that the new project did not compromise any safety issues. LCD decided to positively market the new service to their customers by encouraging them to be environmentally friendly and by earmarking the funds for local community projects.

In detail – Implementing and operating

For the effective implementation of an EMS the organization needs to develop the capabilities and support mechanisms necessary to achieve its environmental objectives and targets. The organization should focus and align its people, strategy, resources and structure towards this aim.

Implementation can be approached in stages, depending on the availability of resources, and the level of awareness of what needs to be done.

ISO 14031(8) can be a useful tool for identifying performance indicators that can demonstrate continual improvement in management and operational functions. This is a guidance document that assists in identifying key performance indicators that can be used for assessing the output from the organization (Management Performance Indicators (MPIs)) and the operational activities (Operational Performance Indicators (OPIs)) of an organization with respect to addressing its impacts on the environment (Environmental Condition Indicators (ECIs)).

Resources – human, physical and financial

The appropriate human, technical (e.g. facilities, equipment) and financial resources need to be made available. In allocating resources, organizations can develop procedures to track the benefits as well as the costs of their environmental activities.

Where the availability of resources is a constraint the organization might consider sharing with others such areas as facilities, technology, knowledge and costs. Examples of this cooperation might be through strategies with organizations in the same supply chain, locality, or industry sector. Trade Associations or similar bodies often act as a focus to support and coordinate developments for its member organizations.

Alignment and integration

Wherever possible, the elements designed to manage environmental issues should be aligned and integrated within the overall management system of the organization. Management system elements that can benefit from integration include:

- organization policies;
- resource allocation;
- operational controls and documentation;
- information and support systems;
- training and development;
- organization and accountability structures;
- reward and appraisal systems;
- measuring and monitoring systems;
- communication and reporting.

A process is necessary to balance and resolve any conflicts between environmental and other business objectives and priorities.

Accountability and responsibility

Commitment from the highest level in the organization is essential and is best demonstrated by ensuring that someone at the most senior level has the specific responsibility for ensuring that the EMS is implemented and operating effectively.

At every level of the organization, people need to be aware of their roles and their responsibilities and to whom they are accountable. More specifically:

- responsibilities should be clearly defined and where job descriptions and work instructions are used they should be considered for inclusion;
- everyone should be given the authority, training and resources (including time) necessary to carry out their responsibilities;
- appropriate arrangements should exist for ensuring everyone is accountable for discharging their responsibilities;
- reporting relationships should be clear and unambiguous;
- where personal appraisal systems exist, environmental performance should be included.

Below is a sample model for developing environmental responsibilities. Organizations will need to define environmental responsibilities based upon their size, structure and circumstances. In smaller organizations the owner is likely to play a wider role as the responsible person.

Environmental responsibility	**Typical person(s) responsible**
Establish overall direction	Chair, Chief Executive, Board of Directors
Develop environmental policy	Chair, Chief Executive. Director responsible for environmental matters
Develop environmental objectives, targets and programmes	Relevant managers

Monitor overall EMS performance	Director responsible
Assure regulatory compliance	Senior Operating Manager
Ensure continual improvement	All managers
Identify customers' expectations	Sales and marketing staff
Identify suppliers' expectations	Purchasers, buyers
Develop and maintain accounting procedures	Finance Manager
Comply with defined procedures	All staff

Environmental awareness and motivation

It is the commitment of the individuals within the organization that transforms the EMS into an effective process. Top management has a key role in building awareness and motivating employees by explaining the organization's environmental values and stressing its commitment to the environmental policy. Everyone should understand, accept and share the environmental values of the organization. Those responsible for achieving environmental objectives and targets should understand and accept the importance of the task.

Motivation of employees to continually improve can be enhanced by recognizing their success in achieving environmental objectives and targets, and by encouraging them to make suggestions that can lead to improvements in environmental performance. Staff suggestion programmes with a scale of rewards can help to gain staff involvement.

Knowledge, skills and training

At all levels in the organization employees should have the knowledge and skills to perform the duties assigned to them. This includes contractors and others working at the site. They must also understand the impact that their activities can have on the environment if not performed correctly.

Training programmes typically cover the following elements:

- identifying employee training needs;
- developing a training plan to address those needs;
- verifying conformance of the training programme to regulatory or organizational requirements;
- training target employee groups;
- documenting and tracking the training received;
- evaluating the training received;
- reviewing and modifying training plans.

Examples of the types of environmental training that can be provided by the organization are as follows:

Type of training	**Audience**	**Purpose**
Raising awareness of the strategic importance of environmental management	Senior managers	To gain commitment and alignment to the organization's environmental policy
Raising general environmental awareness	All employees	To gain commitment to the environmental policy, objectives and targets of the organization, and instil a sense of individual responsibility

Skills enhancement	Employees with environmental responsibilities	To improve performance in specific areas of the organization, e.g. operations, research and development, and engineering
Compliance	Employees whose actions can affect compliance	To ensure regulatory and internal requirements for training are met

Communication and reporting

Arrangements are required to communicate and report information internally and, where desired, externally on the environmental activities of the organization. These arrangements should cover:

- receiving and responding to employee concerns about environmental matters;
- receiving and considering the concerns of other interested parties;
- communicating the organization's environmental policy and performance;
- communicating the results from EMS audits and reviews to those within the organization responsible for performance.

It is important to remember that for both internal and external environmental communication and reporting:

- two-way communication should be encouraged;
- information should be understandable and adequately explained;
- information should be verifiable;
- the organization should present an accurate picture of its performance;
- information should be presented in a consistent form (e.g. similar units of measurement to allow for comparison between one period and another).

An organization can communicate environmental information in a variety of ways:

- externally through an annual report, website, regulatory submissions, public and government records, industry association publications, the media, and paid advertising;
- by organizing open days and publicizing telephone numbers where complaints and questions can be directed;
- internally, through bulletin board postings, internal newspapers, meetings and e-mail messages.

The following items can be included in annual reports:

- organization's profile, including range of products and services;
- environmental policy, objectives and targets;
- environmental management processes (including interested party involvement and employee recognition);
- environmental performance evaluation (including releases, resource conservation, compliance, product stewardship and risk);
- opportunities for improvement;
- supplementary information, such as glossaries;
- independent verification of the contents.

EMS documentation

There is a need for operational processes and procedures to be defined and documented to ensure those responsible for achieving the environmental targets and objectives are aware of what is required. The nature of the documentation should reflect the particular size, complexity and needs of the organization. It should support the EMS, not drive it. Documentation, whether hard copy or computer based, should be readily available and easily understood by all those who need access to it in order to carry out their job roles.

Where elements of the EMS are integrated into the overall management system, the EMS documentation should be integrated into existing documentation. Examples of areas where duplication of information and recording may be avoided include:

- training;
- organizational structure;
- operational procedures;
- emergency contingency plans;
- process/service records and information.

Arrangements should be made to ensure all documentation is:

- dated (including any revisions);
- retained for a specified period;
- identified with the appropriate organization, division, function, activity, and/or contact person;
- periodically reviewed, revised as necessary and approved by authorized personnel prior to issue;
- removed promptly when it becomes obsolete.

Finally, producing a summary or index of the EMS documentation can be useful as a reference guide to the implementation and maintenance of the EMS.

Operational control

Establishing and maintaining effective operational procedures and controls are essential to ensuring the successful implementation of the EMS. When developing or modifying operational procedures and controls the organization should consider the different operations and activities contributing to its significant environmental impacts. These may include:

- research and development;
- design and engineering (not forgetting architects);
- purchasing;
- contracting;
- handling and storage of raw materials;
- production and maintenance processes;
- laboratories;
- storage of products;
- transportation;
- marketing, advertising;
- customer service;
- acquisition, construction or modification of property and facilities.

To help in this process, activities can be divided into three categories:

1. those that prevent pollution and conserve resources in new capital projects, process changes and resources management, property (acquisitions, divestitures and property management), and new products and packaging;
2 those at a daily management level that assure conformance to internal and external organizational requirements, and to ensure their efficiency and effectiveness;
3. those at a strategic level that anticipate and respond to changing environmental and societal requirements or expectations.

Emergency preparedness and response

Contingency plans need to be defined and maintained to mitigate the effects of environmental incidents and potential emergency situations. The types of situation that need to be considered include:

- accidental emissions to the atmosphere;
- accidental discharges to water and land;

- specific environment and ecosystem effects from accidental releases, fire, explosion, natural events (earthquakes, volcanoes, etc.).

Apart from normal operating conditions, the plans need to consider incidents arising, or likely to arise, as a consequence of abnormal operating conditions, accidents or emergency situations, including natural disasters such as floods or fires. Emergency plans can include:

- emergency organization and responsibilities;
- a list of key personnel;
- details of emergency services (e.g. fire stations, spill clean-up services);
- internal and external communication plans;
- actions taken in the event of different types of emergencies;
- information on hazardous materials, including each material's potential impact on the environment, and measures to be taken in the event of accidental release;
- training plans and their periodic testing for effectiveness.

8

Checking

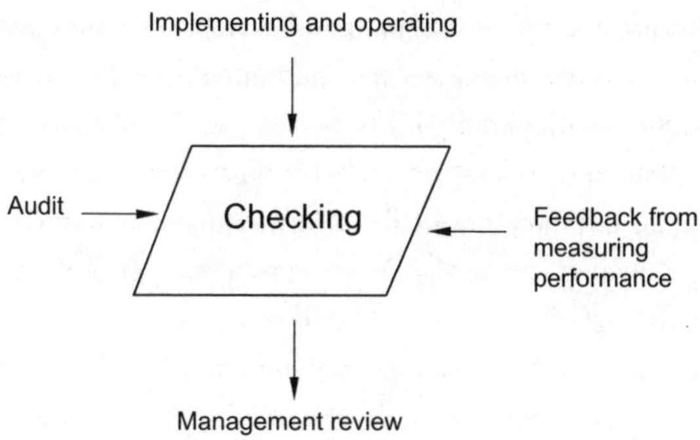

Figure 8.1

Key Elements – Checking

To ensure an effective checking and correcting stage in an EMS, ISO 14001 identifies five areas that need to be addressed:

1. Monitoring and measurement.
2. Evaluation of compliance.
3. Nonconformity, corrective action and preventive action.
4. Control of records.
5. Internal audit (see Chapter 9).

1. Monitoring and measurement

The organization shall establish, implement and maintain a procedure(s) to monitor and measure, on a regular basis, the key characteristics of its operations that can have a significant environmental impact. The procedure(s) shall include the documenting of information to monitor performance, applicable operational controls and conformity with the organization's environmental objectives and targets.

The organization shall ensure that calibrated or verified monitoring and measurement equipment is used and maintained and shall retain associated records. (4.5.1)

Regular monitoring and measuring of actual performance and operational processes against the organization's environmental objectives and targets is an essential routine within an EMS. The results should be analysed and used to ensure compliance with legal and other requirements, determine areas of success, and areas requiring corrective or preventive action and improvement.

Choosing objective and verifiable environmental performance indicators (such as those suggested in ISO 14031) and ensuring the reliability and accuracy of data are the cornerstones to maintaining credibility and avoiding situations that may compromise the organization, particularly where the results are communicated to external interested parties.

2. Evaluation of compliance

Consistent with its commitment to compliance, the organization shall establish, implement and maintain a procedure(s) for periodically evaluating compliance with applicable legal requirements.

The organization shall keep records of the results of the periodic evaluations. (4.5.2.1)

The organization shall evaluate compliance with other requirements to which it subscribes. The organization may wish to combine this evaluation with the evaluation of legal compliance referred to in 4.5.2.1 or to establish a separate procedure(s).

The organization shall keep records of the results of the periodic evaluations. (4.5.2.2)

This is an area that was not particularly well managed by those organizations adopting ISO 14001:1996 and this has necessitated significant changes to assist interpretation.

It is obviously not sufficient to establish compliance when first implementing the system. This is a dynamic process like the rest of the elements in the PDCA process. Records should be kept of conformance or relevant permits. Here again it should be noted that the term 'applicable legal requirements' requires a wider study than just specifically environmental regulations. In addition there is a need to regularly up date the requirements of stakeholders that the organization have taken on-board.

3. Nonconformity, corrective action and preventive action

The organization shall establish, implement and maintain a procedure(s) for dealing with actual and potential nonconformity(ies) and for taking corrective action and preventive action. The procedure(s) shall define requirements for

a) identifying and correcting nonconformity(ies) and taking action(s) to mitigate their environmental impacts;
b) investigating nonconformity(ies), determining their cause(s) and taking actions in order to avoid their recurrence;
c) evaluating the need for action(s) to prevent nonconformity(ies) and implementing appropriate actions designed to avoid their occurrence;
d) recording the results of corrective action(s) and preventive action(s) taken; and
e) reviewing the effectiveness of corrective action(s) and preventive action(s) taken.

Actions taken shall be appropriate to the magnitude of the problems and the environmental impacts encountered.

The organization shall ensure that any necessary changes are made to environmental management system documentation. (4.5.3)

Depending on the circumstances, investigating and correcting nonconformance may be accomplished readily, or it may be a more complex and long-term process requiring formal planning. Either way, the aim is to identify the fundamental reasons behind any deficiencies before deciding on what action is necessary. Reactive, short-term solutions, although expedient, may not address the root cause of the problem and can result in further difficulties in the longer term. See the end of this chapter 'In practice' for a process to help to determine the root cause.

4. Control of records

The organization shall establish and maintain records as necessary to demonstrate conformity to the requirements of its environmental management system and of this International Standard, and the results achieved.

The organization shall establish, implement and maintain a procedure(s) for the identification, storage, protection, retrieval, retention and disposal of records. Records shall be and remain legible, identifiable and traceable. (4.5.4)

The organization should focus on those records needed for implementing and operating the EMS and for recording the extent to which objectives and targets have been met, which can include the following (as listed in Annex A of ISO 14001):

a) complaint records,
b) training records;
c) process monitoring records;
d) inspection, maintenance and calibration records;
e) pertinent contractor and supplier records;
f) incident reports;
g) records of tests for emergency preparedness;
h) audit results;
i) management review results;
j) external communications decision;
k) records of applicable legal requirements;
l) records of significant environmental aspects;
m) records of environmental meetings;
n) environmental performance information;

o) legal compliance records; and

p) communications with interested parties.

Proper account should be taken of confidential information.
Note: Records are not the sole source of evidence to demonstrate conformity to this International Standard. (A.5.4)

Checklist 8.1 identifies the key issues (other than audit) for checking and correcting the EMS. A tick box is provided for you to identify those arrangements you already have in place [1], and those that you need to introduce [2].

CHECKLIST 8.1: Checking the EMS in your organization

1	2	
		Monitoring and measurement
❑	❑	Regular monitoring and measurement of environmental performance is taking place
❑	❑	Procedures exist for verifying the reliability of data
❑	❑	Environmental performance indicators are used to evaluate and compare performance against objectives and targets and other criteria
		Evaluation of compliance
❑	❑	Regular evaluation (at least once a year) of changes to regulations are made
❑	❑	Stakeholders needs are reviewed on a regular basis
❑	❑	The organization evaluates its compliance with applicable legal requirements
		Nonconformity, corrective action and preventive action
❑	❑	Where performance is not meeting criteria, procedures exist for investigating the root causes and taking appropriate corrective action
		Records
❑	❑	Procedures exist for keeping records necessary to implement and operate the EMS and record the extent to which objectives and targets are met
❑	❑	Records are retained for sufficient time periods to satisfy legal requirements and to provide the appropriate level of defence against any environmental or financial liability arising from a nonconformity

In practice – Checking

F&L – Office

The first audit of F&L identified that although there was a new policy on transport, this was not adequately documented. In particular, their contract with the supplier of leased cars did not contain F&L's key environmental requirements. The corrective action was to include a clause in all F&L's contracts with suppliers to address this shortcoming.

The checking process identified that although the water management system was working well, the system had failed to identify that there was no need for automatic flushing of the urinals at the weekend. This situation was corrected by a number of key actions.

UE – Engineering workshop

UE introduced a regular programme of inspection and monitoring using two-people teams. The teams usually comprised a senior manager and an employee 'at the sharp end', both of whom had received some basic training.

During a routine inspection, it became apparent that the procedures for disposal were not being followed. Although there were clearly marked skips for the various sorts of waste, the decorators were found to have disposed of paint residues and waste in a skip intended for waste metal. Immediate corrective action was taken, and an investigation was carried out to establish whether the shortfalls had arisen in the procedures, the documentation, or in the supervision of the decorators. It was established that the fault lay in a failure to clearly define responsibilities in this key area of control.

LCD – Retail

A key area of control is maintaining adequate documentary records and LCD found itself in difficulties when visited by the Environmental Health Officer. It was asked to demonstrate that it was disposing of its waste in an approved manner, and was not responsible for the nearby litter. To its embarrassment, the transfer notes were not being filed and there was no system for recording the collection of waste. These issues needed to be addressed quickly and a system implemented to ensure that they were satisfied that the waste-handlers were working as required by the duty-of-care regulations. This incident also emphasized the need for effective checking systems to ensure that they were complying with all applicable legislation.

Dealing with packaging was identified as not conforming with the regulations, although these had been introduced a year earlier. An immediate action plan was set up to identify what packaging they received and the arrangements they needed (if any) to implement the requirements.

In detail – Checking

To ensure that the EMS is operating as envisaged at the planning stage it is essential to check it by measuring, monitoring and evaluating environmental performance on a regular basis.

1. Monitoring and measurement

There should be a system in place for monitoring and measuring actual performance and operational processes against the organization's environmental objectives and targets, including compliance with legal and other requirements (see below). There is a need to make observations that can be quantitative and qualitative. The results should be analysed and used to determine areas of success, and to identify any activities requiring corrective or preventive action and improvement.

Data should be collected systematically from appropriate sources at a frequency consistent with the environmental objectives, targets and other performance criteria, including the significance of the environmental aspects. To ensure reliability and accuracy, data collection procedures should be supported by quality control and quality assurance practices such as calibration of instruments, use of test equipment, and software and hardware sampling.

There are many areas that can be observed and some examples are given below:

- monitoring emissions;
- monitoring consumption of materials, energy and water;
- checking that waste is being disposed of as specified including checking the contracted waste carrier;
- interviews and observations;
- inspection tours;
- inventory and production records;
- financial and accounting records;
- scientific reports and studies;
- government agencies, academic institutions, etc;
- suppliers and subcontractors.

When setting objectives and targets the organization should consider identifying environmental performance indicators. Indicators provide a means of presenting quantitative and qualitative data or information in a more understandable and useful form. Progress towards achieving environmental objectives and targets can then be measured and reported to interested parties using the selected environmental performance indicator.

Environmental performance indicators must be:

- relevant to the activities, products and services of the organization;
- consistent with environmental policy;
- objective;
- understandable;
- measurable;

- verifiable;
- cost-effective;
- technologically feasible.

Some simple examples of environmental performance indicators are:

- Materials used per unit of production.
- Recycled or re-used materials used.
- Energy used per customer.
- Energy saved due to energy conservation measures.
- Water used per unit of production.
- Water re-used in the production process.
- Emissions to air per unit of production.
- Material discharged to water per unit of production.
- Waste produced per unit of production.
- Percentage waste recycled.
- Degree of compliance with regulations.
- Research and development spending on environmental projects.
- Return on investment of environmental improvement projects.
- Sponsorship of community environmental programmes.

For those seeking more information on selecting and using indicators, ISO 14031, *Environmental management – Environmental performance evaluation – Guidelines,* and ISO/TR14032, *Environmental management – Environmental performance evaluation – Case studies illustrating the use of ISO 14031,* containing EPE case studies, are recommended for further reference.

2. Evaluation of compliance

It is essential to establish, implement and maintain a procedure for evaluating compliance with legal requirements such as permits and licences. This also applies to other requirements to which the organization subscribes.

The organization should establish the frequency and methodology of the evaluation depending on what is required to demonstrate compliance. This process may be integrated with other assessment activities such as quality assurance checks and health and safety assessments.

There are many ways to evaluate compliance, including:

a) audits;
b) document and/or records review;
c) facility inspections;
d) interviews;
e) project or work reviews;
f) routine sample analysis or test results, and/or verification sampling/testing; and
g) facility tour and/or direct observation.

3. Nonconformity, corrective action and preventive action

Nonconformity is non-fulfilment of a requirement. This may relate either to the environmental management system not functioning as intended, or the environmental performance requirements not being met.

Examples of such situations are:

1. system performance:
   a) failure to establish environmental objectives and targets;
   b) failure to define responsibilities, such as those for achieving objectives and targets or for emergency preparedness and response; and
   c) failure to periodically evaluate compliance with legal requirements.
2. environmental performance:
   a) energy reduction targets are not being achieved;
   b) maintenance requirements are not being performed as scheduled; and
   c) operating criteria (e.g. permitted limits) are not being met.

There is a need for a systematic method for determining actual and potential areas of nonconformity, making corrections and taking corrective and preventive action, preferably preventing problems before they occur.

The aim is to identify the root causes of any nonconformance in order to ensure that any necessary action is accurately targeted (see 'Incident Investigation' below).

4. Control of records

Records are evidence of the ongoing operation of the EMS. They are required to track performance and other data necessary to achieve environmental objectives and targets, and to enable employees to fulfil their responsibilities. The organization needs to consider what environmental information and records it needs to keep in order for its EMS to operate effectively. These records and information should include:

- details of nonconformities;
- legislative and regulatory requirements; and other requirements;
- information on compliance and applicable legal requirements;
- permits, consents and authorizations;
- environmental aspects and their associated impacts;
- supplier and contractor information;
- environmental audits and management reviews;
- training;
- monitoring data;
- inspection, calibration and maintenance;
- product identification, composition and property data;
- significant communications with regulators.

It is also necessary in some cases to record all the processes used on the site, now and in the past. These processes may give rise to pollution issues that become of concern only at a later date.

Even when the need for information is kept to a minimum a complex range can still result. Effective management of these records is essential to the successful implementation of the EMS. It should include identifying, collecting, indexing, filing, storing, retrieval, retention and disposal of pertinent EMS documentation and records.

Incident investigation

There are very few occasions where incidents occur that could not have not been foreseen and therefore prevented. Either a similar event had occurred before without harm occurring or someone had knowledge of it within the organization but preventive action had not been taken. The steady drip of a tap is unlikely to improve, but if left unattended it may well lead to a major leak.

For every serious accident there are typically 300 incidents. This is why it is important that we understand the root cause of near misses and incidents where the situation could have had far more serious consequences. A minor spillage on a hard surface is readily manageable whereas such a leak into a nearby stream could be catastrophic.

The Incident Investigation Form included at the end of this chapter should help when investigating the root causes of these events.

There are a number of factors that can be the root cause. It is rare that it is just one. The factors can be analysed into three groups:

1. Personal factors – skill, knowledge, competence, behaviour, etc.
2. Job factors – inappropriate environment, equipment, materials, work instructions, etc.
3. Management organizational factors – shortfalls in policy, resources, supervision, assessment of competency and training needs, etc.

In order to deal with investigations successfully, you will need to have people trained or experienced in this field. The needs obviously should reflect the significance of the event. Equipment, such as cameras, tape measures, torches, sample containers may need to be used and effective systems of communication if the site being investigated is hazardous.

The following plan of action is based on one given in BS 8800:2004 for investigating occupational health and safety incidents but provides a useful checklist of what should be covered when investigating incidents.

Each of these stages needs to be given careful consideration and the amount of time and effort devoted to the investigation should be determined prior to commencement if possible. This should be proportionate to the harm or potential harm caused.

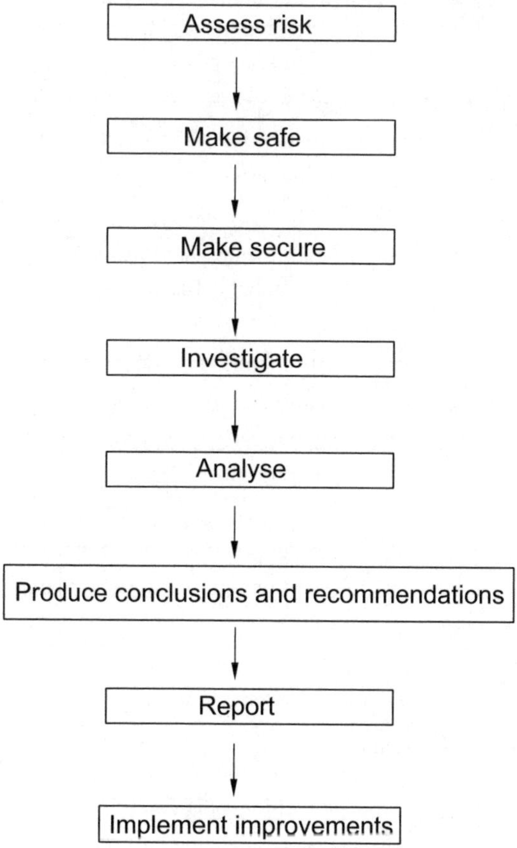

Figure 8.2

There are important issues to be addressed in such investigations. If the facts are to be established it is important that those interviewed feel they are helping rather than being assessed to establish who can be 'blamed' for the event. The organization needs to be seen as one wishing to understand and improve rather than blaming individuals.

Incident Investigation Form

Personal Details (should an individual be involved)		
Name (in full): Employee Number:	DoB: / /	Sex: Male [ ] Female [ ]
Location/Department: Telephone Number: Line Manager:	Home Address: Postcode: Telephone Number:	
Job Description:		
Employment Full Time [ ] Part Time [ ]	Employee [ ] Self-Employed [ ] Contractor [ ] Passer-by [ ] Visitor [ ]	

Event Details			
Date Occurred: / /		Time occurred: Hrs.	
Location/Address where event occurred:			
How did it happen (where appropriate, attach diagrams, photographs, etc.)? Include a brief description of events/period leading up to it:			
Weather conditions at the time:			
Immediate action taken, including action taken to protect others:			
		By Whom:	

Event Details					
Did the event require the emergency services to be summoned? Yes [ ] No [ ]					
Environment Agency advised? Details:			Where:		
Alternative Work (give details below):					
1 Witnesses Name(s):			Location:	Tel No.:	
2 Witnesses Name(s):			Location:	Tel No.:	
3 Witnesses Name(s):			Location:	Tel No.:	
Employee Signature:			Print Name:		
Completed By:			Date completed:		
Date Received by Environmental System Manager:					
Environmental System Manager Signature:					
Incident Status:			Minor [ ]	Major [ ]	
Incident Book Entry/Ref:	Yes [ ]	No [ ]			
Internal Investigation Required?			Yes [ ]	No [ ]	

Investigation
Where did the event happen?
Who and what was affected?
Was there any damage?

Investigation
What was being carried out at the time of the event?
How did the event occur?
Was there anything unusual about the working conditions when the event occurred?
If there was a known risk, was a risk assessment in place – provide a copy?
Were there any external influences that contributed to the event taking place – the materials, plant equipment, working environment etc.?
Were the persons present trained/competent to be undertaking their tasks?
Were there any unusual difficulties encountered whilst the work was being undertaken?
Was the activity under any direct supervision?
Were control measures being used as required?

Investigation
Are there any other factors to be recorded?

Analysis
What are the reasons for the event occurring?
Where there any underlying root causes that led to or contributed to the event?
Has a similar/identical event occurred before – provide details and action taken?
What new control measures are recommended?
1
2
3
4

Analysis			
Are there similar conditions applying elsewhere which should be investigated?			
Which revised control measures should be implemented?			
Control Measure	Completion Date	Person Responsible	Completion Confirmed
1			
2			
Which risk assessments, safety plans need to be reviewed – what is required?			
Action Plan Risk Assessment	Completion Date	Person Responsible	Completion Confirmed
1			
2			
Is any further investigation/action required?			

What was the cost of the event – include lost time, production, reporting and investigation involvement, remedial action costs		
Lost Time	Hours	Value (£)
Production		
Reporting Time – all parties	Hours	Value (£)
Investigation Time – all parties	Hours	Value (£)

<table>
<tr><th colspan="7">Analysis</th></tr>
<tr><td colspan="4">Direct remedial action costs</td><td colspan="3">£</td></tr>
<tr><td colspan="4">Indirect remedial action cots</td><td colspan="3">£</td></tr>
<tr><td colspan="4">Other costs</td><td colspan="3">£</td></tr>
<tr><td colspan="7">Details:</td></tr>
<tr><td colspan="7">Who needs to be advised of the findings and recommendations?</td></tr>
<tr><td colspan="3">Person</td><td colspan="2">Position</td><td colspan="2">Date Completed</td></tr>
<tr><td colspan="3">1</td><td colspan="2"></td><td colspan="2"></td></tr>
<tr><td colspan="3">2</td><td colspan="2"></td><td colspan="2"></td></tr>
<tr><td colspan="3">3</td><td colspan="2"></td><td colspan="2"></td></tr>
<tr><td colspan="7">Review required?</td></tr>
<tr><td>When?</td><td colspan="3"></td><td colspan="2">By whom?</td><td></td></tr>
<tr><td colspan="2">Investigation carried out by
– state all parties:</td><td colspan="5"></td></tr>
<tr><td colspan="2">Signed:</td><td colspan="5"></td></tr>
</table>

9

Auditing

THE STAGES IN ESTABLISHING AN AUDIT SYSTEM

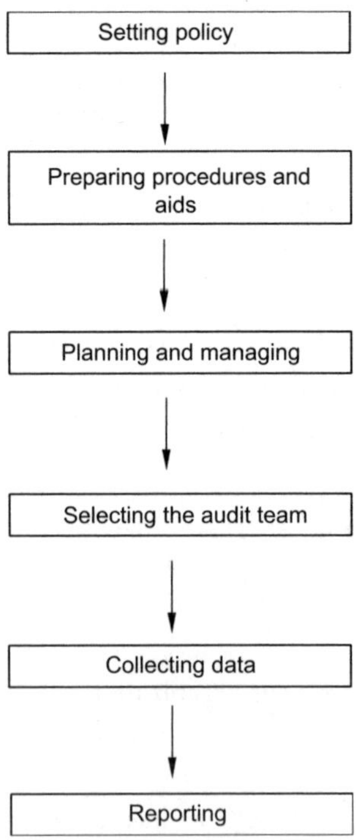

Figure 9.1

Key Elements – Auditing

A system for routinely monitoring environmental performance is insufficient in itself to ensure that the EMS is effective. ISO14001 identifies the need for a further mechanism:

The organization shall ensure that internal audits of the environmental management system are conducted at planned intervals to

a) determine whether the environmental management system
   1) conforms to planned arrangements for environmental management...; and
   2) has been properly implemented and is maintained; and
b) provide information on the results of audits to management. (4.5.5)

The frequency and depth of the audit should be appropriate to the activity being considered. Adopting an audit programme that reflects the environmental importance of the activity concerned and the findings of previous audits, is the best way to ensure its effectiveness.

Audits can be a comprehensive assessment of the EMS or address selected areas or specific topics depending on what is felt to be necessary.

Personnel from within the organization can undertake audits. To maintain credibility it is essential that the auditor is competent, objective and impartial. Competency is essential to provide confidence as to the reliability that can be placed on the audit results. Impartiality is best demonstrated by selecting an auditor who has no responsibility for the activity being audited.

Checklist 9.1 shows the key issues in auditing the EMS. A tick box is provided for you to identify those arrangements you already have in place (1), and those that you need to introduce (2).

CHECKLIST 9.1: Auditing in your organization

1	2	
❑	❑	Periodic audits of the EMS are taking place
❑	❑	Employees conducting audits are competent to perform this task

- ❑ ❑ Employees conducting audits are independent from the activity being audited
- ❑ ❑ Audits confirm whether or not the EMS conforms to planned arrangements for environmental management
- ❑ ❑ Audits confirm the EMS has been properly implemented and maintained
- ❑ ❑ Audits identify strengths and weaknesses in the EMS
- ❑ ❑ Audits verify that the organization is achieving its EMS objectives and targets
- ❑ ❑ Audit results are communicated to all relevant personnel
- ❑ ❑ Audit results are the basis for corrective action
- ❑ ❑ Audit findings are discussed as part of the management review

In practice – Auditing

The three organizations are no longer separate in their approach to environmental management and each has to carry out audits to ensure that their EMS is effective.

The depth and complexity of the audit should be commensurate with the particular organization. For instance, F&L with fewer environmental impacts will simplify the level of audit required. In contrast, for UE, and to a lesser degree LCD, the audits will need to be more complex because of the wider range of activities and processes, and the potential seriousness of their environmental impacts.

In detail – Auditing

Auditing is an essential element of the EMS. Senior managers should be fully committed to its concept, and act reasonably and promptly on any findings and recommendations. The audit should be seen as a positive step and not as a threat. It is essential that everyone cooperates fully and is open and honest with the auditor.

Only by gaining this total cooperation and commitment, can auditing be effective in contributing to the overall continuing success of the system.

The stages in establishing an audit system are as follows:

1. Setting policy

In developing an audit policy the issues that need to be considered include:

a) the objectives and purpose of auditing;
b) the procedures, standards and aids to be used, including the development of checklists, nonconformance reports, etc;
c) who is competent to undertake audits (or be part of the team);
d) the arrangements for the management of the audit, including budget provisions;
e) the audit programme;
f) the format of audit reports and arrangements for responding to them;
g) performance standards for planning and implementation of the audit programme and arrangements for its monitoring;
h) the arrangements for the review of the audit policy, its implementation and for revision as necessary.

2. Preparing procedures and aids

Establishing a procedure for the audit enables it to be undertaken efficiently and smoothly. Those who are being audited may see it as intrusive and time consuming and so it is important for it to be well organized and focused on the issues in hand. A well-prepared audit will determine the facts quickly, giving a productive output that identifies the benefits of the process to those involved.

Issues to consider in preparing for the audit are:

a) the elements of the audit process, preparation, on-site work and follow-up programme;
b) the key elements of the EMS and other key topics that the audit programme will address and the criteria against which the performance will be judged;

c) the means for ensuring that the audit includes a representative sample of activities;
d) how key questions should be framed;
e) the need for auditing aids, e.g. *aide-memoires*, checklists, inspection procedures.

Note: The various checklists found in this book could form the foundation of an audit checklist.

The final form of the audit system should be based on current best practice and be appropriate to the nature and complexity of the organization. An example of what might be included in an assessment programme is given at the end of this chapter.

3. Planning and managing

Audits can be disruptive in a busy organization and any disruption costs incurred are in addition to the direct costs of the audit. It is important, therefore, that a senior person is responsible for planning and managing the audit, including control of the financial budget. Approval for the budget and the audit programme should be obtained prior to commencement.

The programme and frequency of audits should be appropriate to the nature of the environmental aspects, potential impacts, etc. Records of previous audits can be useful in targeting effort towards issues that have previously given cause for concern.

Planning should embrace:

a) preparing the programme, including scheduling of interviews and departmental visits;
b) the scope of the audit;
c) establishing the terms of reference;
d) establishing the timetable;
e) selecting an appropriate audit team.

4. Selecting the audit team

Apart from being competent, it is essential that the auditors are independent and have no direct vested interest in the performance of the area being audited. This can be achieved by using external auditors but usually at a greater cost than using internal staff. The organization needs to decide whether it has sufficient competent and independent staff to undertake the task. One solution is to use an independent senior manager as the lead auditor, using support as required by selecting a team from parts of the organization not being audited. This should ensure a common approach while maintaining the necessary independence. It is important, however, to ensure that the teams selected are competent to audit the areas concerned.

5. Collecting data

There are a number of stages involved including:

a) carrying out structured interviews with key personnel and others throughout the business area to determine that robust procedures are in place, understood and followed. This may seem straightforward but in practice it is essential to ensure that the information collected reflects the actual practices, not what the auditee wants the auditor to see;
b) examining relevant documentation – policy statements, environmental aspect reports, audit records, manuals, etc;
c) carrying out inspections to establish the veracity of the statements made and documentation examined;
d) data analysis;
e) interpretation of data; and
f) maintaining records.

Problems and stress can arise from uncooperative and negative attitudes towards audits. The process needs to be carefully managed to defuse such situations and ensure data is collected with the minimum of fuss and inconvenience to those involved.

Situations may come to light that need immediate attention, or are beyond the competence of the audit team. These should be referred immediately to the audit manager or lead auditor for action.

6. Reporting

Having completed the audit, there is a need to interpret the data and report the results as quickly as possible.

The interpretation will depend on a number of factors including:

a) the competence of the auditors;
b) the experience of the auditors;
c) the integrity of those involved in all aspects of the audit.

To reduce the risk of errors at this stage, it is recommended that checks be built in, wherever possible. This should avoid misrepresentation and misapplication.

The auditors need to be confident of their findings and assist in providing direction for cost-effective remedial action in those areas where there are deficiencies.

The report itself needs to be accurate and confidential. In the first instance, the report should be given to those who commissioned the work, drawing particular attention to those areas where there is a need for immediate action. This can usefully be followed by direct dialogue with those who were interviewed during the audit to review the best way forward. The results should be used in the Reviewing, Planning, and Implementation and Operation stages to determine the most appropriate action.

Issues that might well be covered in an audit

Evidence relating to 'implementation and operation' could include:

- documentation of roles and responsibilities, including organograms;
- level of understanding of responsibilities and the EMS;
- level of resources (human, technological and financial) for the implementation and control of the EMS;

- formal appointing of management representative;
- conducting training needs analyses;
- completion of training programmes;
- level of awareness and competency of employees;
- extent of communication activities (top down, bottom-up and lateral/cross function), both internal and external, using cross-section of employees, not just management;
- documentation of core elements of EMS (paper or electronic form);
- extent of document control;
- carrying out of operational activities in accordance with documented procedures (where the absence of procedures could lead to deviations from the environmental policy, objectives and targets);
- existence of procedures for identifying and responding to emergencies and testing of such procedures.

Evidence relating to 'checking and corrective action' could include:

- documented procedures to monitor and measure key characteristics of operations and evaluate regulatory compliance;
- information to track performance;
- records of information on performance and conformance with policy, objectives and targets;
- calibration records;
- accounts of impact assessments carried out;
- definition of responsibilities/authority for dealing with nonconformities;
- records of corrective action taken or changes in procedures resulting from corrective action;
- process for managing records;
- records needed to demonstrate conformance with requirements such as:
    - information on applicable environmental laws or other requirements;
    - complaint records and handling;
    - training records;
    - product process information;
    - product information;
    - inspection, maintenance and calibration records;

    - pertinent contractor and supplier information;
    - incident reports;
    - information on emergency preparedness and response;
    - records of significant environmental impacts;
    - audit results;
    - management reviews.
- legibility, retrievability and traceability of records;
- definition of record retention times;
- whether periodic audits taken place/and audit schedules documented.

For those seeking more information on environmental auditing ISO 19011:2002 *Guidelines on quality and environmental management systems auditing* (4) is recommended for further reference.

10

Reviewing

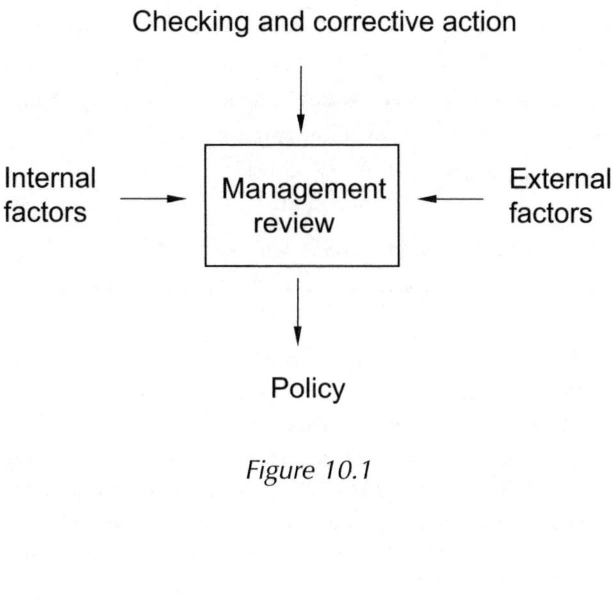

Figure 10.1

Key Elements – Reviewing

In order to ensure a robust EMS, ISO 14001 identifies the need for a periodic management review:

Top management shall review the organization's environmental management system, at planned intervals, to ensure its continuing suitability, adequacy and effectiveness. Reviews shall include assessing opportunities for improvement and the need for changes to the environmental management system, including the environmental policy and environmental objectives and targets. Records of the management reviews shall be retained (4.6)

Although the scope of the review should be comprehensive, not all elements of the EMS need to be reviewed at once, and the process may take place over a period of time. A full management review should be carried out at least every year, particularly for those organizations seeking certification in order to demonstrate their conformance to the standard.

The management review is more strategic and wider in its focus than the EMS audit. For example, although the audit may conclude that everything is in place to meet environmental policy and objectives, the management review may determine that internal or external considerations justify a change.

Checklist 10.1 shows the key issues in reviewing the EMS. A tick box is provided for you to identify those issues you are already addressing [1], and those you need to consider [2].

CHECKLIST 10.1: Reviewing the EMS in your organization

1	2	
❑	❑	Top management carry out periodic reviews of the EMS, at least once every year
❑	❑	Observations, conclusions and recommendations are documented
❑	❑	The review is forward looking, adopting a proactive and strategic approach to improving the EMS and overall business performance
❑	❑	The review assesses the continued suitability of the EMS to meet changing internal and external circumstances and any relevant communications received.
❑	❑	The review assesses the continued suitability of the EMS in delivering continual improvement in environmental performance

- ☐ ☐ The review considers the results of audits and evaluations of compliance with legal and other requirements; the status of corrective and preventive actions; and follow up actions from previous management reviews
- ☐ ☐ The review considers the views of relevant interested parties, including complainants
- ☐ ☐ The review considers the environmental performance of the organization, the extent to which objectives and targets have been met and if any changes are necessary

In practice – Reviewing

The key to success for each organization is how they are managing change relating to environmental management. In each case the management review should initiate a proactive response. A purely reactive response may be a sign that the EMS is failing.

F&L – Office

For F&L the review process should normally be straightforward. However, they are considering diversification into a new business area. Depending on the choice of investment F&L recognize that, if this involves significant impacts on the environment, it could compromise their public image. As part of the planning for this new business, F&L need to formulate their policy on ethical investment.

UE – Engineering workshop

For UE the situation is totally different. In an engineering workshop, because of the developments in systems and technology, the management reviews will need to be more regular to monitor these changes. They will also need to anticipate and respond to any pressures from customers for environmental improvements. UE decided to take an active role in their trade association to ensure that they kept abreast of developments and impending changes to legislation.

LCD – Retail

The diversity of LCD's activities and the interface with the public and visitors means that they will need to be continuously alert to changes, particularly relating to occupational health and safety matters. For instance, wider scares relating to hygiene at retail outlets may require LCD to review their practices to decide whether any further investment and/or training needs to be considered. LCD identified that the IPPC regulations necessitated a fresh look at the organization's strategy on food handling and disposal.

In detail – Reviewing

In essence, the management review should consider the overall EMS against what the organization is aiming to achieve, and decide what further action may be necessary to remedy any shortfalls. The aim of the organization should be to continually improve its EMS to achieve overall improvement in environmental performance.

There are close parallels with the initial environmental review, in that both are aiming to determine where the organization is, where it wants to be and how it is going to get there. In this case, however, the framework of the system (at least the basic information system) is already in place. Here the aim is to consider if the present arrangements will enable the organization to achieve its overall environmental goals. Moreover, the management review should be more proactive in seeking ways to continually improve environmental performance even further, and enhance business performance to the advantage of all stakeholders. It may be important to be ahead of the competition and to be seen as a market leader.

The review should be broad and strategic in its scope, considering the environmental dimensions of all activities, products or services, including their impact on financial performance and possible competitive position. The approach should be proactive, wherever possible, reviewing developments and changes in equipment, working practices, etc., at the earliest possible stage, thus avoiding a reactive response when changes are implemented.

Identifying opportunities for improvement should be central to the management review. Often the process of identifying, analysing and understanding the root causes of deficiencies in the EMS can provide opportunities for future improvement.

The review should not be carried out in isolation from other management disciplines as this can be counterproductive. There is little point, for instance, in solving an environmental problem with, say, solvents, if the water-based alternative causes production and/or quality and/or health and safety problems.

Checklist 10.2 provides a guide (though not exhaustive) to some of the sources of information that the management review should consider. A tick box is provided for you to identify those that you already cover [1], and those you may wish to consider [2].

CHECKLIST 10.2: Sources of information for consideration in the management review

1	2	
❑	❑	Environmental policy
❑	❑	Environmental objectives, targets and performance against them
❑	❑	Findings and recommendations of EMS audits
❑	❑	Results of environmental aspect reviews
❑	❑	Amendments/changes to regulations and legislation
❑	❑	Potential impact of emerging legislation (e.g. EC directives)
❑	❑	New or revised codes of practice/guidance from the EA, trade association, etc.
❑	❑	New or amended instructions/warnings from suppliers of equipment, materials, etc.

- ❑ ❑ Information from press reports, environmental literature, competitors etc.
- ❑ ❑ Information from environmental studies

- ❑ ❑ Changes (present and future) to internal organizational/structure/staffing
- ❑ ❑ Changes (present and future) to the products/services supplied by or to the organization
- ❑ ❑ Changes (present and future) in activities, equipment, plant, buildings, infrastructure, etc.
- ❑ ❑ Information on environmental performance of similar organizations
- ❑ ❑ Staff suggestions and concerns
- ❑ ❑ Competence reports/training needs
- ❑ ❑ Reports from other management disciplines such as quality and OH&S
- ❑ ❑ Trends in accident/incident statistics
- ❑ ❑ Results of investigations into environmental incidents
- ❑ ❑ Achievement of existing objectives and targets, and the setting of new ones
- ❑ ❑ Expectations, requirements and views of interested parties
- ❑ ❑ Advances in science and technology
- ❑ ❑ Market preferences

11

Integrating your Management Systems

Most organizations have a number of management systems operating, some formal and some informal. A difficulty experienced by many organizations is ensuring that these separate systems, such as those for managing quality, environment and occupational health and safety, are fully embedded into their operations. Too often they appear as a peripheral attachment. Every one of these systems should be operating as an integral part of the overall business of managing the organization.

The manager responsible for the EMS cannot be expected to manage the environmental aspects of the organization in isolation. This should be seen as a support resource to the management team. Managers have many issues that they need to manage and these need to be seen as an integral part of the overall management system. Organizations therefore need to recognize that these individual formal management systems are part of an overall management system. This need not be limited to the fields of quality, environment and OH&S, but can also include, for example, financial and human resource management. The aim should be a single defined approach that meets the organization's overall business management needs.

Integration of an EMS can best be achieved by having an integrated business management system or adopting the integrated management system (IMS) approach. Although the IMS approach may seem obvious, there has long been a perceived barrier against progressing towards an integrated system when organizations have adopted formal management systems such as ISO 9001 or ISO 14001. This is because the approaches in the documented systems appear to differ, and the terms and definitions used have also sometimes been different. This has made it difficult for some organizations to determine what they need to do to make it happen.

In fact, there is no real incompatibility between the systems. Although the needs of every organization differ, adopting the IMS approach should satisfy any organization, no matter what systems they currently operate. The framework shown later in this chapter can be used as a structure for the implementation of an integrated system. The basic model was developed as an 'ideal framework' for standards writers. It has been expanded in the publications *IMS: The framework* (9) and *IMS: Implementing and operating* (10) to cover many of the formal systems in use. It has been successfully implemented in a number of organizations both large and small.

It is suggested that organizations wishing to adopt the IMS approach use one of their existing systems as a starting point. This would normally be the system most established and understood and, perhaps, already subject to certification. This system should be reviewed against the framework and any deficiencies identified and rectified. This then becomes the foundation upon which the other management systems are integrated, using common processes, documentation, etc. as appropriate.

The IMS approach is best followed against a structured time frame and a set of deliverable targets. There may be resistance to the IMS approach, usually from those wishing either to protect or promote the design of their own system. It should be made clear that all elements are working to achieve the same overall aim of the effective and efficient management of the organization.

More about the IMS framework

The IMS framework was developed internationally as an idealized model for standards writers who are charged with writing management systems standards. It was seen as being entirely compatible with the management of any area within the organization thus enabling all systems to be aligned. This is shown diagrammatically in the following pages, where the individual management systems are so portrayed that the compatible elements can be merged and much of the redundancy that exists removed.

The framework shown is an expanded version of what was produced for standards writers as an idealized model and is, ideally, aimed at those well-versed in management systems. The requirements or best practices covered in ISO 14001 can, however, be easily accommodated, subject to minor expansion, with the elements in the table. For instance, 2.1 covers the identification and management of environmental aspects and their associated impacts, and legal requirements.

As a starting point, the elements in the table can be used as a checklist to identify to what extent the organization's existing arrangements satisfy the framework, or where there may be shortfalls in these arrangements. Detailed information on the IMS approach and its implementation is available in the IMS series of books, published by BSI, which give guidance on integrating management systems in a number of different fields.

The IMS framework table

Main themes that are common to all MSS	Elements	Typical issues to be covered	ISO 9000: 2000	ISO 14001: 2004	OHSAS 18001
1. Policy	1.1 Policy and principles 1.1 Policy and principles	1.1 The organization needs to have a single policy to demonstrate its commitment to meeting the overall requirements of a management system standard.	5.1 5.3	4.2	4.2
2. Planning	2.1 Identification of needs, requirements and analysis of critical issues.	2.1 The organization needs to identify the issues which have to be controlled and/or improved in order to satisfy the relevant interested party(ies). The term "requirements" includes legal requirements.	5.2 5.4.2 7.2.1 7.2.2	4.3.1 4.3.2	4.3.1 4.3.2

Main themes that are common to all MSS	Elements	Typical issues to be covered	ISO 9000: 2000	ISO 14001: 2004	OHSAS 18001
	2.2 Selection of significant issues to be addressed	2.2 It is recognized that the process described in 2.1 may identify many issues and that these may need to be prioritized.			
	2.3 Setting of objectives and targets	2.3 This section identifies the need to identify clear objectives and targets based on the output of 2.2, the organization's policy and the result from management review (6).	5.4.1	4.3.3	4.3.3
	2.4 Identification of resources	2.4 This outlines the need to ensure that adequate human, infrastructure and financial resources are in place.	5.4.2	4.3.4	4.3.4

Main themes that are common to all MSS	Elements	Typical issues to be covered	ISO 9000: 2000	ISO 14001: 2004	OHSAS 18001
	2.5 Identification of organizational structure, roles, responsibilities and authorities	2.5 The identification of the roles, responsibilities, authorities and their interrelationships within the organization may be needed to ensure effective and efficient operations.	5.5.2 5.5.3	4.4.1	4.4.1
	2.6 Planning of operational processes	2.6 The planning arrangements for the operational processes may include actions affecting how the objectives and targets defined in 2.3 are achieved.	7.1	4.4.6	4.4.6
	2.7 Contingency preparedness for foreseeable events	2.7 The arrangements that need to be in place to manage foreseeable emergencies.	8.3	4.4.7	4.4.7

Main themes that are common to all MSS	Elements	Typical issues to be covered	ISO 9000: 2000	ISO 14001: 2004	OHSAS 18001
3. Implementation and Operation	3.1 Operational Control	3.1 The operational control measures needed to implement the plan(s) and maintain control of activities against defined targets.	7.2 – 7.5	4.4.6	4.4.6
	3.2 Management of human resources	3.2 The management of employees, contractors, temporary staff, etc. (including qualification and activities such as awareness building and training).	6.2.2	4.4.2 4.4.6	4.4.2 4.4.6
	3.3 Management of other resources	3.3 The operational management and maintenance of infrastructure, plant, facilities, finances, etc. which have an impact on the organization's performance.		4.4.6	4.4.6 4.4.4

Main themes that are common to all MSS	Elements	Typical issues to be covered	ISO 9000: 2000	ISO 14001: 2004	OHSAS 18001
	3.4 Documentation and its control	3.4 The management of those documents which are essential to the successful implementation and operation of the management systems.	6.1	4.4.4 4.5.4	4.4.5 4.5.3
	3.5 Communication	3.5 The arrangements for communications both within the organization and from/to external sources.	5.5.3	4.4.3	4.4.3
	3.6 Relationship with suppliers and contractors	3.6 The formalizing of arrangements for those who supply and contract their services to the organization which have an impact on the organization's performance.	7.4	4.4.6	4.4.5

Main themes that are common to all MSS	Elements	Typical issues to be covered	ISO 9000: 2000	ISO 14001: 2004	OHSAS 18001
4. Performance Assessment	4.1 Monitoring and Measuring	4.1 The mechanism by which the organization assesses its performance.	8.2	4.5.1	4.5.1
	4.2 Analysing and handling nonconformities	4.2 The determination of nonconformities and the manner in which these are dealt with.	8.3	4.5.2 4.5.3	4.5.2
	4.3 System audits	4.3 The system audit of the management system.	8.2.2	4.5.5	4.5.4
5. Improvement	5.1 Corrective action	5.1 The mechanism for eliminating the causes of nonconformities both in the management system and the operational processes.	8.5.2	4.5.3	4.5.2

Main themes that are common to all MSS	Elements	Typical issues to be covered	ISO 9000: 2000	ISO 14001: 2004	OHSAS 18001
	5.2 Preventive action	5.2 The mechanism for instigating action to prevent future nonconformities of both the management system and the operational processes	8.5.3	4.5.3	4.5.2
	5.3 Continual improvement	5.3 The provisions made for continual improvement of the management system.	5.4.2 8.5.1		
6. Management Review	6.1 Management Review	6.1 Management mechanism to review the system to ensure its continuing suitability, adequacy and effectiveness, instruct improvements and new directions when found necessary.	5.6	4.6	4.6

Appendix 1

Self-assessment Questionnaire

How to use this questionnaire

There follows a series of questions covering the various aspects of environmental management in your organization. For each of the questions two answers are offered, numbered (1) and (4), which describe the two extreme positions your organization may have. If your organization occupies the 'middle ground', tick 2 if nearer to 1 and 3 if nearer to 4. Tick one number for each question.

Once you have answered each question, enter your score in the 'Assessment of Performance' at the end, total the score, then see how your organization rates.

a. Management commitment

Does your organization recognize environmental management as an integral part of business performance by allocating responsibility at the most senior level for ensuring continual improvement in environmental performance?

1. There is no clear management responsibility.
4. We have defined and documented responsibility and authority for environmental management. Ultimate responsibility is allocated to a manager at the most senior level but everyone is actively involved and encouraged in the continual improvement of environmental performance.

a.	**1**	**2**	**3**	**4**

b. Policy

Does your organization define and document its environmental policy?

1. We do not have an environmental policy.
4. We have a comprehensive and documented policy that clearly defines the organization's commitment to the environment. It is communicated to all persons working for and on behalf of the organization, and is available to the public. It expresses a clear commitment by top management to continual improvement of environmental performance.

b.	**1**	**2**	**3**	**4**

c. Resources

Does your organization provide adequate resources to environmental management?

1. We do not allocate any resources.
4. We allocate a budget and resources to ensure continual cost-effective improvement in environmental performance.

c.	**1**	**2**	**3**	**4**

d. Environmental aspects

Has your organization identified its environmental aspects?

1. We have not identified our environmental aspects.
4. We identify our significant environmental aspects through a comprehensive assessment programme covering all our activities, products and services. The significant aspects are prioritized and considered in setting our environmental objectives and targets.

d.	**1**	**2**	**3**	**4**

e. Legal and other requirements

Does your organization identify all legal and other requirements to which the organization subscribes related to its environmental aspects?

1. We have little knowledge about legislation that might apply to our activities.
4. We operate procedures and implement controls to ensure full regulatory compliance.

e.	**1**	**2**	**3**	**4**

f. Best practice

Does your organization identify and embrace any codes of practice and/or other guidance relevant to its activities, products and services?

1. We have no knowledge about codes of practice or other guidance that may be relevant to our activities.
4. We have embraced within our procedures what we consider to be the best practice on the basis of relevant guidance from the Environmental Agency, industrial associations, professional bodies, suppliers etc.

f.	**1**	**2**	**3**	**4**

g. Objectives and targets

Does your organization set objectives and targets to ensure continual improvement of environmental performance?

1. We never set objectives or targets.
4. We set and publish objectives and targets consistent with our policy to ensure continual improvement of environmental performance and these are regularly reviewed.

g.	1	2	3	4

h. Employee responsibility

Does the organization assign environmental responsibility to its employees?

1. We do not assign any environmental responsibility to our employees.
4. Every employee is aware of their responsibilities with respect to environmental management as it applies within their field of operation.

h.	1	2	3	4

i. Training, awareness and competence

Does your organization carry out training to increase the awareness of employees about environmental issues?

1. We do not have any environmental training.
4. We have a continual training programme to ensure our employees are aware of environmental issues and, where necessary, about their own role and responsibilities. Employees are competent to carry out specific tasks that may affect environmental performance.

i.	1	2	3	4

j. Internal communication

Does your organization provide information about environmental matters to employees?

1. We do not provide employees with information on any environmental issue.
4. We have an established communication system to keep employees informed about environmental issues, including policy, objectives and targets, performance, remedial actions and future plans.

j.	1	2	3	4

k. External communication

Does your organization have a procedure for receiving, documenting and responding to relevant communications from external interested parties?

1. We do not have any such system.
4. We have established procedures to respond to such communications.

k.	1	2	3	4

l. Information

Does your organization have a system for gathering relevant environmental information?

1. We do not have a system.
4. We maintain a system, appropriate to the organization, for gathering relevant environmental information and for keeping records of environmental performance.

l.	1	2	3	4

m. Operational control

Does your organization embrace environmental issues in its operational control system?

1. We focus exclusively on 'business' issues, e.g. products, processes or services.
4. We integrate environmental issues into every procedure and instruction covering our activities, processes and tasks.

m.	**1**	**2**	**3**	**4**

n. Emergency response

Does your organization have a procedure(s) for responding to accidents and emergency situations, and for preventing or mitigating the environmental impacts that they may cause?

1. We do not have any procedures for responding to emergency situations.
4. We have an emergency response plan, which includes preventing or minimizing any environmental impacts. Employees are aware of their role and responsibilities in implementing the plan.

n.	**1**	**2**	**3**	**4**

o. Audits

Does your organization carry out audits of its environmental activities?

1. We do not carry out audits.
4. We have a programme of regular audits of our environmental management system undertaken by at least one auditor who is both competent and independent. Remedial action is initiated where deficiencies are found.

o.	**1**	**2**	**3**	**4**

p. Management review

Does your organization carry out management reviews of its environmental activities?

1. We do not carry out management reviews.
4. We undertake regular reviews using a designated senior manager to ensure the suitability, efficiency and effectiveness of our environmental management system. The review considers audit results, environmental performance and other relevant internal/external factors, including overall business performance.

p.	**1**	**2**	**3**	**4**

Assessment of performance

TOPIC	SCORE			
	1	2	3	4
a. Management commitment				
b. Policy				
c. Resources				
d. Environmental aspects				
e. Legal and other requirements				
f. Best practice				
g. Objectives and targets				
h. Employee responsibility				
i. Training, awareness and competence				
j. Internal communication				
k. External communication				
l. Information				
m. Operational control				
n. Emergency response				
o. Audits				
p. Management review				
Total:				
Overall performance:				

Performance rating

Score

16-20 Your organization has presently little commitment to environmental management and you need to review urgently your situation. You may be in breach of current UK environmental legislation, as well as occupational health and safety legislation and, therefore, open to prosecution.

21–48 A level of environmental management exists but full commitment by the organization does not. You need to consider carefully building upon those areas where you are presently weak and moving towards a comprehensive environmental management system.

49–64 Provided you score not less than 3 in any area your organization has a comprehensive environmental management system in place. This should not invite complacency, and continuous management and development of the system should be a high priority of the organization.

Appendix 2

Keeping up to date with environmental legislation and regulations

There is a massive amount of legislation on environmental matters to which businesses have to conform. It is constantly being added to and amended, and in some cases is different depending upon which part of the UK you are operating in. Therefore, any list of applicable regulations will quickly become out of date, and large parts of it will be irrelevant to any particular business.

Fortunately, there is a solution to this problem which is free of charge and readily available so long as you have access to the internet.

The Environment Agency maintains an excellent website devoted to "helping small and medium sized enterprises in the UK to understand the complex environmental regulations that can affect them". The web address is www.netregs.gov.uk.

This website has guidelines which lead you to the regulations which will apply to your business depending on the kind of activities which you carry out and in which part of the UK your business is.

There are four main areas in the site:

1) Sector guidelines

These are guidelines for the business sector you are operating in, such as Chemical Manufacture, Electronics, or Hotels and Restaurants. Not every type of activity is listed, but those on Office Businesses, for example, will apply to almost all businesses to some degree. It lists all the activities involved in office operations, with links to guidance on Resource Management (waste, energy, water), and Storage and Handling of Materials, as well as good practice guidance on Transport, Purchasing, etc. There are also links to Envirowise Guides which contain good practice guidelines on numerous different activities, some of which are almost certain to be relevant to your business.

2) Management guidelines

This is a good starting point for new users as it covers the environmental legislation that may apply to different aspects of your business. You can look at legislation relating to particular aspects, such as emissions to air, packaging or water. There are checklists which can lead to the legislation that is relevant to you, making it clear what regulations you need to know about. You can also look at a complete list of all the management guidelines, with subjects arranged alphabetically from Animal By-Products through to Water Efficiency.

3) Legislation

This gives the key pieces of environmental legislation that will be relevant to your business. It is divided into two sections; current legislation and future legislation. It is the current legislation that you have to check first to see what applies to you here and now. It varies depending on where in the UK you are operating, i.e. if you are in England, click on 'English Legislation'. This leads to a subject list and the principal legislation which applies in each. The list of current English legislation is reproduced on the following pages. Those in Scotland or Northern Ireland need to check on the specific controls that apply to them.

There is also a section explaining the difference between legislation - the basic acts of parliament which give authority in principle, and the detailed regulations which are made to give practical effect to them. In most cases you will be able to access and, if you wish, print off the actual acts and regulations themselves.

The site also gives notice of likely future legislation, whether arising from the EU, from the UK government or consultation in progress. This can be invaluable in giving advance warning of developments so that businesses can prepare for them. This can save a lot of trouble and expense.

All this is free of charge. There are also links to further sources of help and information if you should need it.

The site is regularly maintained and while it does not claim to be fully comprehensive and current on all regulations it is for practical purposes by far the best source of guidance for most businesses.

4) More resources

The fourth section gives various other sources of information.

In many business sectors, trade associations issue similar guidance for their members on environmental issues particularly relevant to their activities, e.g. the Engineering Employers' Federation. Full use should be made of these facilities where they exist. If you are not sure of what is available, this section provides a link to the Trade Association Forum which gives a full list.

There should be one nominated person within your business who is given the responsibility of keeping abreast of applicable environmental legislation and making sure that management is aware of what exists and what is expected to arrive shortly.

Current legislation applicable in England

1	2	3	Air Legislation
❑	❑	❑	Clean Air Act 1993
❑	❑	❑	Environmental Protection Act 1990
❑	❑	❑	Pollution Prevention and Control Act 1999
❑	❑	❑	Crop Residues (Burning) Regulations 1993, SI 1366
❑	❑	❑	Environmental Protection (Controls on Ozone-Depleting Substances) Regulations 2002, SI 528
❑	❑	❑	Genetically Modified Organisms (Contained Use) Regulations 2000, SI 2831
❑	❑	❑	Genetically Modified Organisms (Contained Use) (Amendment) Regulations 2002, SI 63
❑	❑	❑	Genetically Modified Organisms (Deliberate Release) Regulations 2002, SI 2443

❑ ❑ ❑ Genetically Modified Organisms (Deliberate Release) (Amendment) Regulations 2004, SI 2411

❑ ❑ ❑ Greenhouse Gas Emissions Trading Scheme Regulations 2005, SI 925

❑ ❑ ❑ Non-Road Mobile Machinery (Emission of Gaseous and Particulate Pollutants) Regulations 1999, SI 1053

❑ ❑ ❑ Non-Road Mobile Machinery (Emission of Gaseous and Particulate Pollutants) (Amendment) Regulations 2004, SI 2034

❑ ❑ ❑ Notification of Cooling Towers and Evaporative Condensers Regulations 1992, SI 2225

❑ ❑ ❑ Smoke Control Areas (Authorised Fuels) (England) Regulations 2001, SI 3745

❑ ❑ ❑ Smoke Control Areas (Authorised Fuels) (England) (Amendment) Regulations 2002, SI 3046

❑ ❑ ❑ Smoke Control Areas (Exempted Fireplaces) (England) Order 2003, SI 2328

❑ ❑ ❑ Solvent Emissions (England and Wales) Regulations 2004, SI 107

1 2 3 Chemicals Legislation

❑ ❑ ❑ Batteries and Accumulators (Containing Dangerous Substances) Regulations 1994, SI 232

❑ ❑ ❑ Batteries and Accumulators (Containing Dangerous Substances) (Amendment) Regulations 2000, SI 3097

❑ ❑ ❑ Batteries and Accumulators (Containing Dangerous Substances) (Amendment) Regulations 2001, SI 2551

❑ ❑ ❑ Carriage of Dangerous Goods by Rail Regulations 1996, SI 2089

❑ ❑ ❑ Carriage of Dangerous Goods by Road Regulations 1996, SI 2095

❑ ❑ ❑ Carriage of Dangerous Goods (Amendment) Regulations 1998, SI 2885

❑ ❑ ❑ Chemicals (Hazard Information and Packaging for Supply) Regulations 2002, SI 1689

❑ ❑ ❑ Control of Major Accident Hazards Regulations 1999, SI 743

❑ ❑ ❑ Control of Major Accident Hazards (Amendment) Regulations 2005, SI 1088

❑ ❑ ❑ Dangerous Substances and Preparations (Safety) (Consolidation) and Chemicals (Hazard Information and Packaging for Supply) (Amendment) Regulations 2000, SI 2897

❑ ❑ ❑ Environmental Protection (Controls on Dangerous Substances) Regulations 2003, SI 3274

❑ ❑ ❑ Environmental Protection (Disposal of Polychlorinated Biphenyls & Other Dangerous Substances) (England & Wales) Regulations 2000, SI 1043

❑ ❑ ❑ Environmental Protection (Disposal of Polychlorinated Biphenyls & Other Dangerous Substances) (England and Wales) (Amendment) Regulations 2000, SI 3359

❑ ❑ ❑ Notification of Installations Handling Dangerous Substances Regulations 1982, SI 1357 (not available online)

❑ ❑ ❑ Notification of Installations Handling Dangerous Substances (Amendment) Regulations 2002, SI 2979

❑ ❑ ❑ Notification of New Substances Regulations 1993, SI 3050

❑ ❑ ❑ Planning (Hazardous Substances) Regulations 1992, SI 656

❑ ❑ ❑ Sulphur Content of Liquid Fuels (England and Wales) Regulations 2000, SI 1460

1 2 3 Energy Legislation

❑ ❑ ❑ Buildings Regulations 2000, SI 2531

❑ ❑ ❑ Energy Efficiency (Refrigerators and Freezers) Regulations 1997, SI 1941

❑ ❑ ❑ Energy Information (Combined Washer-Driers) Regulations 1997, SI 1624

❑ ❑ ❑ Energy Information (Dishwashers) Regulations 1999, SI 1676

❑ ❑ ❑ Energy Information (Household Air Conditioners) (No. 2) Regulations 2005, SI 1726

❑ ❑ ❑ Energy Information (Household Electric Ovens) Regulations 2003, SI 751Energy Information (Household Refrigerators and Freezers) Regulations 2004, SI 1468

❑ ❑ ❑ Energy Information (Lamps) Regulations 1999, SI 1517

❑ ❑ ❑ Energy Information (Tumble Driers) Regulations 1996, SI 601

❑ ❑ ❑ Energy Information (Washing Machines) Regulations 1996, SI 600

❑ ❑ ❑ Energy Information (Washing Machines) (Amendment) Regulations 1997, SI 803

❑ ❑ ❑ Energy Information and Energy Efficiency (Miscellaneous Amendments) Regulations 2001, SI 3142

❑ ❑ ❑ Town and Country Planning (Environmental Impact Assessment) (England and Wales) Regulations 1999, SI 293

❑ ❑ ❑ Town and Country Planning (Environmental Impact Assessment) (England and Wales) (Amendment) Regulations 2000, SI 2867

1	2	3	**Land Legislation**
❑	❑	❑	Agricultural Land (Removal of Surface Soil) Act 1953 (not available online)
❑	❑	❑	Countryside and Rights of Way Act 2000
❑	❑	❑	Environment Act 1995
❑	❑	❑	Environmental Protection Act 1990
❑	❑	❑	Wildlife and Countryside Act 1981
❑	❑	❑	Wildlife and Countryside Act 1981 (England and Wales) (Amendment) Regulations 2004, SI 1487
❑	❑	❑	Wildlife and Countryside (Amendment) Act 1985
❑	❑	❑	Wildlife and Countryside (Amendment) Act 1991
❑	❑	❑	Action Programme for Nitrate Vulnerable Zones (England and Wales) Regulations 1998, SI 1202
❑	❑	❑	Animal By-Products Regulations 2003, SI 1482
❑	❑	❑	Contaminated Land (England) Regulations 2000, SI 227
❑	❑	❑	Contaminated Land (England) (Amendment) Regulations 2001, SI 663
❑	❑	❑	Control of Pollution (Silage, Slurry and Agricultural Fuel Oil) Regulations 1991, SI 324
❑	❑	❑	Control of Pollution (Silage, Slurry and Agricultural Fuel Oil) (Amendment) Regulations 1996, SI 2044
❑	❑	❑	Control of Pollution (Silage, Slurry and Agricultural Fuel Oil) (Amendment) Regulations 1997, SI 547
❑	❑	❑	Environmental Impact Assessment (Forestry) (England and Wales) Regulations 1999, SI 2228
❑	❑	❑	Environmental Impact Assessment (Uncultivated Land and Semi-natural Areas) (England) Regulations 2001, SI 3966
❑	❑	❑	Farm Waste Grant (Nitrate Vulnerable Zones) (England) Scheme 2003, SI 562
❑	❑	❑	Nitrate Vulnerable Zones (Additional Designations) (England) (No2) Regulations 2002, SI 2614
❑	❑	❑	Sludge (Use in Agriculture) Regulations 1989, SI 1263
❑	❑	❑	Sludge (Use in Agriculture) (Amendment) Regulations 1990, SI 880

1	2	3	**Noise and Statutory Nuisance Legislation**
❑	❑	❑	Anti-Social Behaviour Act 2003
❑	❑	❑	Civil Aviation Act 1982 (not available online)
❑	❑	❑	Control of Pollution Act 1974 (not available online)
❑	❑	❑	Environmental Protection Act 1990

- ❑ ❑ ❑ Local Government (Miscellaneous Provisions) Act 1982 (not available online)
- ❑ ❑ ❑ Noise Act 1996
- ❑ ❑ ❑ Noise and Statutory Nuisance Act 1993
- ❑ ❑ ❑ Control of Noise (Codes of Practice for Construction and Open Sites) (England) Order 2002, SI 461
- ❑ ❑ ❑ Household Appliances (Noise Emission) Regulations 1990, SI 161
- ❑ ❑ ❑ Household Appliances (Noise Emission) (Amendment) Regulations 1994, SI 1386
- ❑ ❑ ❑ Noise Emission in the Environment by Equipment for Use Outdoors Regulations 2001, SI 1701
- ❑ ❑ ❑ Noise Emission in the Environment by Equipment for Use Outdoors Amendment) Regulations 2001, SI 3958
- ❑ ❑ ❑ Statutory Nuisance (Appeals) Regulations 1995, SI 2644

1 2 3 Pollution Prevention & Control (PPC) Legislation (including IPC)

- ❑ ❑ ❑ Control of Pollution Act 1974 (not available online)
- ❑ ❑ ❑ Environment Act 1995
- ❑ ❑ ❑ Environmental Protection Act 1990
- ❑ ❑ ❑ Pollution Prevention and Control Act 1999
- ❑ ❑ ❑ Environmental Licences (Suspension and Revocation) Regulations 1996, SI 508
- ❑ ❑ ❑ Environmental Protection (Applications, Appeals and Registers) Regulations 1991, SI 507
- ❑ ❑ ❑ Environmental Protection (Applications, Appeals and Registers) (Amendment) Regulations 1996, SI 667
- ❑ ❑ ❑ Environmental Protection (Applications, Appeals and Registers) (Amendment No. 2) Regulations 1996, SI 979
- ❑ ❑ ❑ Environmental Protection (Authorisation of Processes) (Determination Periods) Order 1991, SI 513
- ❑ ❑ ❑ Environmental Protection (Authorisation of Processes) (Determination Periods) (Amendment) Order 1994, SI 2847
- ❑ ❑ ❑ Environmental Protection (Controls on Dangerous Substances) Regulations 2003, SI 3274
- ❑ ❑ ❑ Environmental Protection (Controls on Hexachloroethane) Regulations 2003, SI 602
- ❑ ❑ ❑ Environmental Protection (Controls on Injurious Substances) Regulations 1992, SI 31

❑ ❑ ❑ Environmental Protection (Controls on Injurious Substances) Regulations 1993, SI 1

❑ ❑ ❑ Environmental Protection (Controls on Injurious Substances) (No. 2) Regulations 1993, SI 1643

❑ ❑ ❑ Environmental Protection (Controls on Injurious Substances) Regulations 1999, SI 3244

❑ ❑ ❑ Environmental Protection (Controls on Injurious Substances) (Amendment) Regulations 2001, SI 3141

❑ ❑ ❑ Environmental Protection (Prescribed Processes and Substances) Regulations 1991, SI 472

❑ ❑ ❑ Environmental Protection (Prescribed Processes and Substances) (Amendment) Regulations 1992, SI 614

❑ ❑ ❑ Environmental Protection (Prescribed Processes and Substances) (Amendment) Regulations 1993, SI 1749

❑ ❑ ❑ Environmental Protection (Prescribed Processes and Substances) (Amendment) (No. 2) Regulations 1993, SI 2405

❑ ❑ ❑ Environmental Protection (Prescribed Processes and Substances Etc.) (Amendment) Regulations 1994, SI 1271

❑ ❑ ❑ Environmental Protection (Prescribed Processes and Substances Etc.) (Amendment) (No. 2) Regulations 1994, SI 1329

❑ ❑ ❑ Environmental Protection (Prescribed Processes and Substances) (Amendment) Regulations 1995, SI 3247

❑ ❑ ❑ Environmental Protection (Prescribed Processes and Substances) (Amendment) (Hazardous Waste Incineration) Regulations 1998, SI 767

❑ ❑ ❑ Environmental Protection (Prescribed Processes and Substances Etc.) (Amendment) (Petrol Vapour Recovery) Regulations 1996, SI 2678

❑ ❑ ❑ Pollution Prevention and Control (England and Wales) Regulations 2000, SI 1973

❑ ❑ ❑ Pollution Prevention and Control (England and Wales) (Amendment) Regulations 2001, SI 503

❑ ❑ ❑ Pollution Prevention and Control (England and Wales) (Amendment) Regulations 2002, SI 275

❑ ❑ ❑ Pollution Prevention and Control (England and Wales) (Amendment) (No 2) Regulations 2002, SI 1702

❑ ❑ ❑ Pollution Prevention and Control (England and Wales) (Amendment) Regulations 2003, SI 1699

❑ ❑ ❑ Pollution Prevention and Control (England and Wales) (Amendment) (No. 2) Regulations 2003, SI 3296

❑ ❑ ❑ Pollution Prevention and Control (England and Wales) (Amendment) and Connected Provisions Regulations 2004, SI 3276

❑ ❑ ❑ Pollution Prevention and Control (Unauthorised Part B Processes) (England and Wales) Regulations 2004, SI 434

1 2 3 Plant Protection Legislation

❑ ❑ ❑ Food and Environment Protection Act 1985 (not available online)

❑ ❑ ❑ Pesticides Act 1998

❑ ❑ ❑ Plant Health Act 1967 (not available online)

❑ ❑ ❑ Biocidal Products Regulations 2001, SI 880

❑ ❑ ❑ Biocidal Products (Amendment) Regulations 2003, SI 429

❑ ❑ ❑ Control of Pesticides Regulations 1986, SI 1510 (not available online)

❑ ❑ ❑ Control of Pesticides (Amendment) Regulations 1997, SI 188

❑ ❑ ❑ Plant Health (Great Britain) Order 1993, SI 1320 (as amended)

❑ ❑ ❑ Plant Health (Amendment) (England) Order 2004, SI 2365

❑ ❑ ❑ Plant Protection Products (Basic Conditions) Regulations 1997, SI 189

❑ ❑ ❑ Plant Protection Products Regulations 2003, SI 3241

❑ ❑ ❑ Plant Protection Products (Amendment) Regulations 2004, SI 1810

1 2 3 Radioactive Substances Legislation

❑ ❑ ❑ Radioactive Material (Road Transport) Act 1991

❑ ❑ ❑ Radioactive Substances Act 1993

❑ ❑ ❑ Radioactive Material (Road Transport) Regulations 2002, SI 1093

❑ ❑ ❑ Radioactive Material (Road Transport) (Amendment) Regulations 2003, SI 1867

❑ ❑ ❑ Radioactive Substances (Appeals) Regulations 1990, SI 2504

1 2 3 Waste Legislation

❑ ❑ ❑ Control of Pollution (Amendment) Act 1989

❑ ❑ ❑ Environment Act 1995

❑ ❑ ❑ Environmental Protection Act 1990

❑ ❑ ❑ Controlled Waste Regulations 1992, SI 588

❑ ❑ ❑ Controlled Waste (Amendment) Regulations 1993, SI 566

❑ ❑ ❑ Controlled Waste (Registration of Carriers and Seizure of Vehicles) Regulations 1991, SI 1624

❑ ❑ ❑ Controlled Waste (Registration of Carriers and Seizure of Vehicles) (Amendment) Regulations 1998, SI 605

❑ ❑ ❑ End of Life Vehicles Regulations 2003, SI 2635

❑ ❑ ❑ End-of-Life Vehicles (Producer Responsibility) Regulations 2005, SI 263

❑ ❑ ❑ Environmental Protection (Duty of Care) Regulations 1991, SI 2839

❑ ❑ ❑ Environmental Protection (Duty of Care) (England) (Amendment) Regulations 2003, SI 63

❑ ❑ ❑ Hazardous Waste (England and Wales) Regulations 2005, SI 894

❑ ❑ ❑ Landfill (England and Wales) Regulations 2002, SI 1559

❑ ❑ ❑ Landfill (England and Wales) (Amendment) Regulations 2004, SI 1375

❑ ❑ ❑ Landfill (England and Wales) (Amendment) Regulations 2005, SI 1640

❑ ❑ ❑ List of Wastes (England) Regulations 2005, SI 895

❑ ❑ ❑ List of Wastes (England) (Amendment) Regulations 2005, SI 1673

❑ ❑ ❑ Packaging (Essential Requirements) Regulations 2003, SI 1941

❑ ❑ ❑ Packaging (Essential Requirements) (Amendment) Regulations 2004, SI 1188

❑ ❑ ❑ Producer Responsibility Obligations (Packaging Waste) Regulations 1997, SI 648

❑ ❑ ❑ Producer Responsibility Obligations (Packaging Waste) (Amendment) Regulations 1999, SI 1361

❑ ❑ ❑ Producer Responsibility Obligations (Packaging Waste) (Amendment) (No. 2) Regulations 1999, SI 3447

❑ ❑ ❑ Producer Responsibility Obligations (Packaging Waste) (Amendment) (England and Wales) Regulations 2000, SI 3375

❑ ❑ ❑ Producer Responsibility Obligations (Packaging Waste) (Amendment) (England) Regulations 2002, SI 732

❑ ❑ ❑ Producer Responsibility Obligations (Packaging Waste) (Amendment) (England) Regulations 2003, SI 3294

❑ ❑ ❑ Producer Responsibility Obligations (Packaging Waste) (Amendment) (England and Wales) Regulations 2005, SI 717

❑ ❑ ❑ Special Waste Regulations 1996, SI 972

❑ ❑ ❑ Special Waste (Amendment) Regulations 1996, SI 2019

❑ ❑ ❑ Special Waste (Amendment) Regulations 1997, SI 251

❑ ❑ ❑ Special Waste (Amendment) (England and Wales) Regulations 2001, SI 3148

❑ ❑ ❑ Transfrontier Shipment of Radioactive Waste Regulations 1993, SI 3031

❑ ❑ ❑ Transfrontier Shipment of Waste Regulations 1994, SI 1137

❑ ❑ ❑ Transfrontier Shipment of Waste (Amendment) Regulations 2005 SI 187

❑ ❑ ❑ Waste Incineration (England and Wales) Regulations 2002, SI 2980

❑ ❑ ❑ Waste Management Licences (Consultation and Compensation) Regulations 1999, SI 481

❑ ❑ ❑ Waste Management Licensing Regulations 1994, SI 1056

❑ ❑ ❑ Waste Management Licensing (Amendment) Regulations 1995, SI 288

❑ ❑ ❑ Waste Management Licensing (Amendment No 2) Regulations 1995, SI 1950

❑ ❑ ❑ Waste Management Licensing (Amendment) Regulations 1996, SI 1279

❑ ❑ ❑ Waste Management Licensing (Amendment) Regulations 1997, SI 2203

❑ ❑ ❑ Waste Management Licensing (Amendment) Regulations 1998, SI 606

❑ ❑ ❑ Waste Management Licensing (Amendment) (England) Regulations 2002, SI 674

❑ ❑ ❑ Waste Management Licensing (Amendment) (England) Regulations 2003, SI 595

❑ ❑ ❑ Waste Management Licensing (England and Wales) (Amendment and Related Provisions) (No. 3) Regulations 2005 SI 1728

❑ ❑ ❑ Waste Management Regulations 1996, SI 634

1 2 3 Water Legislation

❑ ❑ ❑ Water Act 2003

❑ ❑ ❑ Water Industry Act 1991

❑ ❑ ❑ Water Industry Act 1999

❑ ❑ ❑ Water Resources Act 1991

❑ ❑ ❑ Anti-Pollution Works Regulations 1999, SI 1006

❑ ❑ ❑ Control of Pollution (Applications, Appeals and Registers) Regulations 1996, SI 2971

❑ ❑ ❑ Control of Pollution (Oil Storage) (England) Regulations 2001 SI 2954

❑ ❑ ❑ Groundwater Regulations 1998, SI 2746

❑ ❑ ❑ Protection of Water Against Agricultural Nitrate Pollution (England and Wales) Regulations 1996, SI 888

❑ ❑ ❑ Water Resources (Environmental Impact Assessment) (England and Wales) Regulations 2003, SI 164

❑ ❑ ❑ Water Supply (Water Quality) Regulations 2000, SI 3184

❑ ❑ ❑ Water Supply (Water Quality) Regulations 2001, SI 3911

❑ ❑ ❑ Water Supply (Water Quality) (Amendment) Regulations 2001, SI 2885

Appendix 3

References and further reading

[1] ISO 14001:2004, *Environmental management systems – Requirements with guidance for use*

[2] ISO 14004:2004, *Environmental management systems – General guidelines on principles, systems and supporting techniques*

[3] BS 8555:2003, *Environmental management systems – Guide to the phased implementation of an environmental management system including the use of environmental performance evaluation*

[4] ISO 19011:2002, *Guidelines for quality and/or environmental management systems auditing*

[5] ISO 9001:2000, *Quality management systems – Requirements*

[6] OHSAS 18001:1999, *Occupational health and safety management systems – Specification*

[7] BS 8800:2004, *Occupational health and safety management systems – Guide*

[8] ISO 14031:1999, *Environmental management – Environmental performance evaluation – Guidelines*

[9] *IMS: The framework,* published by BSI, 2001

[10] *IMS: Implementing and operating,* published by BSI, 2002

ISO 14001 series

The complete ISO 14001 series of publications are as follows:

- ISO 14001:2004, *Environmental management systems – Requirements with guidance for use*
- ISO 14004:2004, *Environmental management systems – General guidelines on principles, systems and supporting techniques*
- ISO 14015:2001, *Environmental Management – Environmental assessment of sites and organizations*
- ISO 14020:2000, *Environmental labels and declarations – General principles*
- ISO 14021:1999, *Environmental labels and declarations – Self-declared environmental claims (Type II environmental labelling)*
- ISO 14024:1999, *Environmental labels and declarations – Type I environmental labelling – Principles and procedures*
- ISO/TR 14025:2000, *Environmental labels and declarations – Type III environmental declarations*
- ISO 14031:1999, *Environmental management – Environmental performance evaluation – Guidelines*
- ISO/TR 14032:1999, *Environmental management – Examples of environmental performance evaluation (EPE)*
- ISO 14040:1997, *Environmental management – Life cycle assessment – Principles and framework*
- ISO 14041:1998, *Environmental management – Life cycle assessment – Goal and scope definition and inventory analysis*
- ISO 14042:2000, *Environmental management – Life cycle assessment – Life cycle impact assessment*
- ISO 14043:2000, *Environmental management – Life cycle assessment – Life cycle interpretation*
- ISO/TR 14047:2003, *Environmental management – Life cycle impact assessment – Examples of application of ISO 14042*
- ISO/TS 14048:2002, *Environmental management – Life cycle assessment – Data documentation format*

- ISO/TR 14049:2000, *Environmental management – Life cycle assessment – Examples of application of ISO 14041 to goal and scope definition and inventory analysis*
- ISO 14050:2002, *Environmental management – Vocabulary*
- ISO/TR 14061:1998, *Information to assist forestry organizations in the use of Environmental Management System standards ISO 14001 and ISO 14004*
- ISO/TR 14062:2002, *Environmental management – Integrating environmental aspects into product design and development*
- ISO Guide 64:1997, *Guide for the inclusion of environmental aspects in product standards*
- ISO 14063*, *Environmental management – Environmental communication – Guidelines and examples*
- ISO 14064-1*, *Greenhouse gases – Part 1: Specification for the quantification, monitoring and reporting of organization emissions and removals*
- ISO 14062-2*, *Greenhouse gases – Part 2: Specification for the quantification, monitoring and reporting of greenhouse gas emission reductions or removal enhancements*
- ISO 14063-3*, *Greenhouse gases – Part 3: Specification and guidance for the validation and verification of greenhouse gas assertion*
- ISO 19011:2002, *Guidelines for quality and/or environmental management systems auditing*

* In preparation.